The
Power
of
Positive
Leadership

How and Why Positive Leaders
Transform Teams and Organizations
and *Change the World*

JON GORDON

WILEY

Library of Congress Cataloging-in-Publication Data:

Names: Gordon, Jon, 1971– author.
Title: The power of positive leadership : how and why positive leaders
    transform teams and organizations and change the world / Jon Gordon.
Description: Hoboken : Wiley, 2017. | Includes bibliographical references and
    index. |
Identifiers: LCCN 2017008997 (print) | LCCN 2017034146 (ebook) |
    ISBN 9781119352037 (ePDF) | ISBN 9781119351702 (epub) |
    ISBN 9781119351979 (hardback)
Subjects: LCSH: Leadership. | Employee motivation. | Organizational change. |
    BISAC: BUSINESS & ECONOMICS / Leadership. | BUSINESS & ECONOMICS /
    Motivational. | BUSINESS & ECONOMICS / Management.
Classification: LCC HD57.7 (ebook) | LCC HD57.7 .G66674 2017 (print) |
    DDC 658.4/092–dc23
LC record available at https://lccn.loc.gov/2017008997

Printed in the United States of America

10 9 8 7 6 5 4

*To Ken Blanchard, for teaching me and showing me
how a true positive leader lives and leads.
Your example and support changed my life and
I am forever grateful.*

Contents

Contents

Contents

Chapter 1

From Negative to Positive

Being positive doesn't just make you better;
it makes everyone around you better.

I 'm not naturally a positive person. People think I am because of my books and talks, but the truth is that I have to work hard to be positive. It doesn't come naturally to me. In fact, I find it ironic that I would write a book like this— and that my life's work centers on the importance of positivity. It's true that we teach what we need to learn. I know that my quest to become a more positive person and better leader has made me a better teacher.

I grew up in Long Island, New York, in a Jewish-Italian family; with a lot of food and a lot of guilt; a lot of wine and a lot of whining. My parents were very loving but they were not the most positive people in the world. My dad was a New York City police officer who worked in undercover narcotics. He fought crime every day and wasn't a big fan of positivity. I remember waking up in the morning and saying, "Good morning, Dad." He would say in his thick New York accent, "What's so good about it?" My dad was Al Bundy before Al Bundy was Al Bundy.

By the age of 31, I was a fearful, negative, stressed-out, and miserable husband and father to two young children. My wife had had enough. She gave me an ultimatum: Change or our marriage was over. I knew she was right that I needed to change. I knew that I was allowing the stress of life and the fear of not being able to provide for my family to get the best of me. I told my wife I would change and began researching ways I could be more positive. At the time, positive psychology was an emerging field, and I read everything I could about it. I began to practice positivity and write about the things I was doing. I met Ken Blanchard, who became my role model. I began taking "thank you" walks to practice gratitude, enjoy the outdoors, and feel grateful instead of stressed. This was a life-changing practice that not only energized me physically, emotionally, and spiritually, but also provided time for many profound insights and ideas to come to me.

One of these ideas was *The Energy Bus*. In case you haven't read it, it's about a guy named George who is miserable and negative. His team at work is in disarray and he has problems at home. George was easy for me to write about because he was based on me and my struggle with negativity and adversity. George wakes up one Monday morning to discover his car has a flat tire and he has to take the bus to work. On the bus, he meets Joy the bus driver, who, along with a cast of characters, teaches George the 10 rules for the *ride of his life*. Their advice not only helps him become a more positive person, but also a better father, husband, and leader at work. On one level, George demonstrates that positivity is a difference maker in business, education, life, and sports. On another level, George represents the fact that every one of us will have to overcome negativity, adversity, and challenges to ultimately define ourselves and our team's success.

Since *The Energy Bus* was published in 2007, I've had the opportunity to work with many Fortune 500 companies, businesses, professional and college sports teams, hospitals, schools, and nonprofits that have utilized the book. I've met many amazing positive leaders and have witnessed firsthand the power of positive leadership. I've seen how they have led, inspired, and transformed their teams and organizations. I've observed the impact they have had and the results they have achieved. I've also researched many positive leaders throughout history and learned about their paths to success. There is indeed a power associated with positive leadership, and my goal with this book is twofold. First, I aim to explain how and why positive leaders make a difference. Second, I intend to provide a simple framework filled with practical ideas that will help anyone become a positive leader. It's one of the most important things a person can do because one positive leader will inspire many others to become positive leaders as well. My daughter wrote her college admission essay last year and it said, "When I was young my mom struggled with her health and my dad struggled with himself. But over the years I watched my dad work to become a more positive person. Then he started writing and speaking about it and sharing his message with others. I saw people change for the better and I know that if he can change, and they can change, the world can change." Her words brought tears to my eyes because I realized that my one decision to be a positive leader not only impacted my life but also my marriage, my children, my team at work, and everyone around me. My hope is that you too will discover the power of positive leadership in your own life. I know that being a positive leader doesn't just make *you* better; it makes everyone around you better. You can start today!

Chapter 2

Real Positive

We are positive, not because life is easy.
We are positive because life can be hard.

I t takes a lot of work to create a world-class organization. It's hard to develop a successful team. It's not easy to build a great culture. It's challenging to work toward a vision and create a positive future. It's difficult to change the world. As a leader, you will face all kinds of challenges, adversity, negativity, and tests. There will be times when it seems as if everything in the world is conspiring against you. There will be moments you'll want to give up. There will be days when your vision seems more like a fantasy than a reality. That's why positive leadership is so essential. When some people hear the term *positive leadership* they roll their eyes because they think I'm talking about Pollyanna positivity, where life is full of unicorns and rainbows. But the truth is that we are not positive because life is easy. We are positive because life can be hard. Positive leadership is not about fake positivity. It is the real stuff that makes great leaders great. Pessimists don't change the world. Critics write words but they don't write the future. Naysayers talk about problems but they don't solve them. Throughout history we see that it's the optimists, the believers, the dreamers, the doers, and the positive leaders who change the world. The future belongs to those who believe in it and have the belief, resilience, positivity, and optimism to overcome all the challenges in order to create it.

Research by Manju Puri and David Robinson, business professors at Duke University, shows that optimistic people work harder, get paid more, are elected to office more often, and win at sports more regularly.[1] Research by psychologist Martin Seligman also shows that optimistic salespeople perform better than their pessimistic counterparts.[2] And psychologist Barbara Fredrickson's research demonstrates that people who experience more positive emotions than negative ones are more likely to see the bigger picture, build relationships, and thrive in their work and career, whereas people who experience mostly negative emotions are more likely to have a narrower perspective and tend to focus more on problems.[3] Daniel Goleman's research demonstrates that positive teams perform at higher levels than negative teams.[4] John Gottman's pioneering research on relationships found that marriages are much more likely to succeed when the couple experiences a five-to-one ratio of positive to negative interactions; when the ratio approaches a one-to-one ratio, marriages are more likely to end in divorce.[5] Additional research also shows that workgroups with positive-to-negative interaction ratios greater than three to one are significantly more productive than teams that do not reach this ratio. Teams with more negative interactions are more likely to be stagnant and unproductive. The positive energy you share with your team is significant. According to Wayne Baker, the research he and Robert Cross conducted shows that "the more you energize people in your workplace, the higher your work performance." Baker says that this occurs because people want to be around you. You attract talent and people are more likely to devote their discretionary time to your projects. They'll offer new ideas, information, and opportunities to you before others.

Baker adds that the opposite is also true. If you de-energize others, people won't go out of their way to work with or help you.[6] Gallup estimates that negativity costs the economy $250–$300 billion a year and affects the morale, performance, and productivity of teams.

The research is clear. Positivity is about more than having a positive state of mind. It's also a life changer and gives people a competitive advantage in business, sports, and politics. While the pessimists are complaining about the future, the energy vampires are sabotaging it, and the realists are talking about it, the optimists are working hard with others to create it. Puri and Robinson's research shows that our attitude helps create a self-fulfilling prophecy. Because optimists believe in a positive future, they actually *delude* themselves into working more to make it possible. Their belief makes them willing to take actions to achieve it. As a result, positive leaders invest their time and energy in driving a positive culture. They create and share the vision for the road ahead. They lead with optimism and belief and address and transform the negativity that too often sabotages teams and organizations. They take on the battle, overcome the negativity, face the adversity, and keep moving forward. They devote all their energy and effort to uniting and connecting their organization and invest in relationships that truly build great teams. They believe in their principles. They believe in their people. They believe in teamwork. They believe in the future. They believe in what's

11

possible, so they act and do, connect and create, build and transform their team and organization—and change the world.

In the following chapters I'm going to take you through a simple, powerful model and framework you can utilize and implement to enhance your leadership capabilities and put your positive leadership into action.

The Framework

Positive Leaders Drive Positive Cultures

Positive Leaders Create and Share a Positive Vision

Positive Leaders Lead with Optimism, Positivity, and Belief

Positive Leaders Confront, Transform, and Remove Negativity

Positive Leaders Create United and Connected Teams

Positive Leaders Build Great Relationships and Teams

Positive Leaders Pursue Excellence

Positive Leaders Lead with Purpose

Positive Leaders Have Grit

Chapter 3

Positive Leaders Drive Positive Cultures

Culture is not just one thing. It's everything.

P ositive leaders drive positive cultures. I use the word *drive* here because as a leader you are the driver of your bus and you have a big role and responsibility in creating the kind of journey you and your team will experience. One year I spoke at a school district and talked with all their leaders, mostly school principals. I shared the same principles and strategies with everyone. At the end of the year, I heard from two principals from the district. One principal had given every member of her staff *The Energy Bus* to read and followed up with staff meetings where she discussed and reinforced the principles each month. She focused all of her energy on creating a positive culture, one meeting, one conversation, one interaction, one positive message, one teacher, and one student at a time. She completely transformed the morale, engagement, energy, and culture of her school. The other principal I heard from was very disappointed and told me that she had handed a copy of *The Energy Bus* to all her teachers, encouraged them to read it, and wondered why it didn't have much of an impact on her school and culture. I realized in that moment that you can give a team a bus, but unless you have drivers, it doesn't move. It's not a book that makes a difference.

It's not a lecture or a keynote. It's the leader that makes the difference. It's the leader that must drive the culture.

Your Most Important Job

Your most important job as a leader is to drive the culture—and not just any culture. You must create a positive culture that energizes and encourages people, fosters connected relationships and great teamwork, empowers and enables people to learn and grow, and provides an opportunity for people to do their best work. Culture is not just one thing; it's everything. Culture drives expectation and beliefs. Expectations and beliefs drive behaviors. Behaviors drive habits. And habits create the future. It all starts with the culture you create and drive throughout the organization. That's where all success and great results begin.

Driving your culture is not something you can delegate. You are the leader and you must spend your time, energy, and effort creating and building the culture of your team and organization. Nancy Koeper, the retired president of UPS for the Northwest Region, made culture her number-one priority as she drove a positive culture through an organization that was, literally, full of drivers. She wanted to improve engagement and morale, so she rolled out *The Energy Bus* to the 1,000 leaders she led with the intent of enhancing positive leadership, positive interactions, and improved relationships with the UPS drivers. Her leaders all read the book, then discussed ways to implement the ideas. They then rolled out *The Energy Bus* to their 11,000 drivers in the district by simply focusing on positivity, positive interactions, and improved relationships. I had yet to have a company measure results after utilizing *The Energy Bus*, so it was exciting to hear from Nancy a year later. She reported that engagement, morale, and performance had risen while disengagement and absenteeism had fallen. Nancy drove the UPS bus and it made all the difference.

Alan Mulally, the former CEO of Ford, led one of the most incredible corporate turnarounds in history. In 2006, when he stepped into the CEO role, the automaker had just suffered an annual loss of $12.7 billion and was on the verge of bankruptcy. In just a few short years under his leadership, Ford was back in the black and the company saw an annual profit every year since 2009. Mulally credited this improbable feat on the organization's focus on driving and building a "One Ford" culture that was centered on the idea of "One Team" where everyone in the organization was committed to the enterprise and to each other. A cultural shift like this doesn't happen by accident. Mulally shared with me his management system, a simple but powerful set of principles, philosophies, behaviors, and processes he designed to create a culture at Ford that fostered unity, teamwork, appreciation, transparency, safety, and even joy. I'll share more of what I learned from Mulally, who defines his leadership as *positive leadership*, throughout the book because he's one of history's greatest examples of positive leadership and he demonstrates that great cultures happen when positive leaders know their most important job is to drive the culture.

Culture Beats Strategy

When Apple was just the two Steves (Jobs and Wozniak), they knew the culture they wanted to create. They would be the culture that challenged the status quo. Everything they did, including hiring people, running campaigns, and creating products, was influenced by this culture. Even after Steve Jobs's death, the culture continues to influence everything they do. It's why Apple is famous for stating the maxim that "culture beats strategy." You have to have the right strategy of course, but it is your culture that will determine whether your strategy is successful. I believe Apple will be successful as long as they innovate and create from the strength of their culture. If they lose their culture they will lose their way and, like many of the mighty that have come before them, they will fall.

Very few people understand the importance of culture more than Rick Hendrick, the owner and founder of Hendrick Automotive Group and Hendrick Motorsports. In a world where there are thousands of car dealerships and many NAS-CAR racing teams, Hendrick Automotive is the largest privately owned dealer group in the United States, and Hendrick Motorsports is the winningest racing organization in the modern NASCAR era. Through speaking to the leaders of Hendrick Automotive and Jimmie Johnson's racing team (owned by Hendrick Motorsports), I have witnessed the incredible culture in both organizations. It's clear that they are driven by the same person. Rick Hendrick's signature leadership and drive are ingrained in everything they do. His people are humble, hungry, thankful, kind, and appreciative. They are on a quest for greatness. Their buildings are spotless. Their energy is always positive and contagious. Everyone wants to be the best and win. When you spend time with two companies— when you see the success of his automotive dealerships and the Jeff Gordon, Jimmie Johnson, and Dale Earnhardt, Jr. racing teams—you realize that culture not only beats strategy, but it also fuels it and drives people and organizations to record growth and performance.

Know What You Stand For

You might be wondering where to start when driving and building a culture. I believe it starts with two questions: 1) What do we stand for? 2) What do we want to be known for? While visiting Hendrick Automotive, I asked several of Rick's leaders what they stood for, and they all said *servant leadership*. They told me that Rick leads the way and, in doing so, puts himself last in every decision he makes for his organization. He is very focused on making sure everyone's voice is heard because it is the team that shapes the company today, tomorrow, and in the future. His executive staff knows that Rick expects them to serve the people they lead in the same way. Teamwork through trust and respect is also one of Hendrick's core organizational values. One of Rick's mantras is *"None of us is as smart as all of us."* He constantly states, "People are our biggest asset! If we take care of our people they will take care of our customers, and if we work together we will all accomplish more." This principle comes to life through weekly and monthly meetings where employees share best practices. Having the high performers share how they win in the market lifts the whole company.

As you would expect, Rick is all about integrity and doing the right thing, doing what you say you will do, and being honest and telling the truth regardless of the situation. Leaders at Hendrick Automotive and Hendrick Motorsports also told me

19

they have a passion for winning and don't give up until they do so. Accountability and commitment to continuous improvement help them improve individually and collectively as a team and organization. They want to be known for their culture and winning ways. They celebrate their past success and make it very clear they expect future success. Yet, despite all their success, they are a culture that believes in developing champions who serve others. They want to be known for making a difference in the lives of others and their community. Hendrick leaders are extremely selective in whom they hire. Only people who fit their culture, embrace the same values, and possess a high level of professionalism are added to the team. Because, as an organization, Hendrick knows what their culture stands for, they are able to choose the right people who fit their culture and who stand for the same things. They also invest heavily to train and develop their people in order to sustain success and retain their talent. Brad Stevens, the head coach of the Boston Celtics, once told me that your culture is not only your tradition, but also the people in the locker room who carry it on. When you have people who fit your culture and carry it on, it comes to life in a powerful way.

I've also had the opportunity to speak to Southwest Airlines a few years ago, and they told me how consultants suggested they charge passengers to check luggage since the competition was doing it and they could make hundreds of millions of dollars in additional revenue. Southwest considered their proposal but in the process asked themselves an important question: *Is this what we stand for?* They went straight to their purpose statement: "To connect People to what's important in their lives through friendly, reliable, and low-cost air travel."

They ultimately decided that if they were for everyday fliers and low-cost air travel, they shouldn't charge baggage fees. You would think they would have missed out on a lot of money, but a funny thing happened. Southwest started to get new customers because the airline didn't charge for bags. They ran advertising campaigns highlighting the fact that bags fly free, and they gained market share in the process. Their revenue grew to new heights. It's a great example that once you know what you stand for, decisions are easy to make. When your culture dictates your decisions, you are on the right path to positive results.

More than Words

Driving a positive, high-performing culture requires more than words. After all, everyone has a mission statement, but only the great organizations also have people who are on a mission. The greatest mission statement in the world is pointless unless your people are on a mission. When I speak to leaders, I always tell them that it doesn't matter what core values you have written on the walls of your building and website if you don't live and breathe them every day. Remember Enron? One of their core values was *integrity*.

As a positive leader, you can't just show the way and talk about the way. You must also *lead* the way. You must live your culture and know that it is an extension of who you are as a leader. If you don't set the example and live the values—if you aren't on a mission—your culture won't come to life. The same goes for the people on your team and in your organization. Everyone creates the culture. Leaders define what your

Positive Leaders Drive Positive Cultures

culture stands for, and your people define whether or not they stand for your culture. Education expert Todd Whitaker says that the unwritten rules in an organization are more important than the written ones. The rules you set with your example are what your organization is really all about, so make sure you live and breathe the values written on the walls. Don't tell the world your mission statement. Show the world you are on a mission. Then energize and empower your people to be culture drivers and culture builders. Positive leaders know they can't do it alone. Culture starts with the leader living it and inspiring and empowering others to live it as well.

Positively Contagious

As a leader, the energy you put into your team and culture determines the quality of it. Research from the HeartMath Institute (www.heartmath.org) shows that when you have a feeling in your heart, it goes to every cell in the body, then outward—and people up to 10 feet away can sense the feelings transmitted by your heart.[7] This means that each day you are broadcasting to your team how you feel. You are broadcasting either negative energy or positive energy, apathy or passion, indifference or purpose. Research from Harvard University also supports the idea that the emotions you feel are contagious and affect the people around you.[8] Your team is just as likely to catch your bad mood as the flu and, on the flip side, they will catch your good mood as well. As a leader your attitude, energy, and leadership is contagious, and it has a big impact on your culture. Great cultures and teams are built with positive, contagious energy, so it's essential that you share those types of feelings. When you walk into the office or the meeting, or onto the field, you have a decision to make: Are you going to be a germ to your team or a big dose of vitamin C? Please know that you don't have to be an extrovert to be positively contagious. Sharing positive energy doesn't mean you have to be a rah-rah leader and bounce off the walls. It means that from the heart you simply broadcast the love, passion, positivity, and purpose that you have for your team, organization, and mission. It comes more from your essence than it does your words. When Winston Churchill was leading Great Britain during WWII in its fight for survival against Hitler, people commented that Churchill looked 20 years younger than he did before the war. During Great Britain's darkest hour, Churchill was energized by the seemingly impossible task before him and his country, and he inspired his nation with passion and contagious energy. His famous words and speeches were a manifestation of his inner strength and conviction.

Create a Culture that People Feel

When I visited West Point in the summer of 2014, the USA Basketball Men's National Team happened to be visiting at the same time. Head coach Mike "Coach K" Krzyzewski brought the team there to understand what it truly means to represent the United States of America. Coach K knew the place was special. After all, he attended West Point, played basketball there under Bob Knight, returned as the head coach after his five years of military service, and coached there for five years before becoming the head coach of Duke University. Coach K knew the players wouldn't fully understand how special the place was by hearing him talk about it. They had to experience and feel it. He said, "You can't talk about this place, see a movie about this place, you have to feel this place. You go to a place like this, you get it." Coach K knew it was the same when talking about service and sacrifice. The players had to feel it, so at the beginning of their visit, Coach K brought the team to the West Point Cemetery, where they had a meeting with family members of fallen soldiers. The players on Team USA listened as the family members told them about their children and how they died serving their country. The players may have understood the concepts of service and sacrifice before, but after seeing the graves of the fallen soldiers, listening to personal stories, and feeling the loss of the family members, they truly got it. It's also a powerful lesson for all of us. Feeling is more powerful than hearing. You can't just create a culture where people hear about what's important. You must create a culture where people feel what's important. You must create a culture where people don't just hear your talk but rather they feel your walk. When they *feel* the mission and also hear about the mission, they'll be on a mission.

Invest in the Root if You Want the Fruit

If culture is so important then why don't more leaders focus on it? It's because culture is not easily quantifiable. You can measure sales. You can measure revenue, costs, profits, goals, wins and losses, outcomes and results, but it's not easy to measure the health and strength of your culture. Culture building also requires a lot of work, time, energy, and focus to drive and sustain it. It's a lot easier to simply measure the fruit of the tree than it is to cultivate the root. The world measures leaders by their results, and this causes many leaders to focus only on the results and outcomes, meaning, they focus on the fruit of the tree and ignore the root. However, we know that if you focus on the fruit and ignore the root, the tree dies. That's not my opinion. It's the truth, and we see it play out all too often on sports teams, businesses, hospitals, schools, churches, and families. If you want the fruit, you must invest in the root. If you invest in the root, you will always receive a great supply of fruit. Of course you should measure your fruit, but you should do so knowing that it's simply a byproduct of how well you are nurturing the root. Your culture is your root, and your focus should be on the process that nourishes and produces the fruit.

In the book *You Win in the Locker Room First*, which I co-wrote with Coach Mike Smith, we discussed how, during his first five years as the head coach of the Atlanta Falcons, he was the second winningest coach in the league, behind only Bill Belichick. But during the next two seasons, he only won 10 total games. What happened? During the fifth season, the Falcons made it to the NFC championship. They were one play and 10 yards away from going to the Super Bowl. They failed to make the play and lost the game, and after that they became an organization that only focused on getting to the Super Bowl.

During Mike's first five years as head coach, the Falcons were simply focused on the process, the culture, the connections, and the relationships in the locker room, including all the little things that made them successful. But during the next two years, everyone in the organization, including Mike, was

Positive Leaders Drive Positive Cultures

focused only on the outcome. If they didn't make it to the Super Bowl, the season would be considered a failure by the media, the fan base, and many within the organization. The pressure was on and everyone in the organization felt it. Mike says he allowed that to steer the Falcons away from the very things that had made the team successful during those five winning years. Mike said he did a poor job of making sure the new members of the team, staff, and organization understood the culture they had worked so hard to create. Everyone learned the hard way that culture can change almost as quickly as the momentum in a football game. Mike says he let outside forces and pressure weaken their culture. The team stopped investing in the root and Mike says the world watched as their tree withered. It was a lesson he would never forget.

You Must Keep Building Your Culture

Mike Smith learned that a culture will not sustain itself. You must sustain it. You must continue to build it, reinforce it, live it, protect it, and fight for it. Positive leaders don't live in a Pollyanna world. They understand that every day there are forces seeking to sabotage their culture and success, and so they work relentlessly to keep it strong. I was recently giving a talk at the American Baseball Coaches Association convention and Kyle Stark, the assistant general manager for the Pittsburgh Pirates, was in the audience. I shared how Kyle was obsessed with culture and always looking for ways to strengthen it. When I saw Kyle after my talk, I apologized for saying he was obsessed. He said, "It's fine. You're right. I am obsessed. It's one of the things that helped us turn this organization around from a perennial loser to a perennial contender and I'm not letting up. I will continue to fight for and build upon what we have built."

I've learned from many of these great leaders that you must invest in your culture in such a way that it becomes stronger than all the forces trying to sabotage it. I've learned that you and your team must value your culture to the point that you will fight for it. I've learned that when you create a culture worth fighting for and invest in your people to the degree that they want to fight for your culture and for each other, your organization will have the grit and strength to overcome the challenges you face and become an unstoppable and positive force.

Chapter 4

Positive Leaders Create and Share a Positive Vision

It's important to have a compelling vision and a comprehensive plan. Positive leadership—conveying the idea that there is always a way forward—is so important because that is what you are here for—to figure out how to move the organization forward.

—Alan Mulally

P ositive leadership is all about seeing and creating a brighter and better future. It's about inventing, innovating, creating, building, improving, and transforming education, healthcare, business, government, technology, farming, design, communities, cities, transportation, and every aspect of our lives and the world we live in. Some scoff when leaders share bold ideas, imaginative goals, and seemingly impossible dreams, but ideas, imagination, and dreams are the fabric positive leaders weave together to create the future and change the world.

At one time, *Star Wars* was just an idea in the mind of George Lucas, but now the Force is as strong as ever. J.K. Rowling had a vision of Harry Potter and now he's an iconic part of our society—and as real as a roller-coaster in Universal Studios. John F. Kennedy had a vision for sending a man to the moon. Ronald Reagan saw the Berlin Wall come down before it crumbled. Steve Jobs imagined the iPod and iPhone long before the world was addicted to them. Abraham Lincoln envisioned a united America. Martin Luther King, Jr., had a dream about equality. George Washington had thoughts of revolution and freedom before fighting for independence.

A positive leader sees what's possible and then takes the next steps to rally and unite people to create it. Every invention, project, creation, and transformation starts with an idea, an imagination, and a vision of what's possible. History shows us that if you can see it, you can create it. If you have a vision, then you also have the power to make it happen. Positive leaders tap into the power of a vision and find a way forward. But in order to rally people to follow you, you must be able to articulate and communicate your vision in a simple, clear, bold, and compelling way. Whether it's Ford's *One Ford*, IBM's *Let's Build a Smarter Planet*, GM's *Design, build and sell the world's best vehicles*, Feeding America's *A hunger-free America*, Alzheimer's Association's a *world without Alzheimer's*, or Fort Bend Independent School District's vision to inspire and equip students to create a *future beyond what students can imagine*, a vision serves as a rallying cry that unites and ignites people. It's not meant to be a novel as long as *War and Peace* or a paragraph filled with buzzwords and jargon that no one understands, remembers, or cares about. It's meant to be simple, memorable, compelling, and exciting. Remember, Martin Luther King, Jr. said, "I have a *dream*." He didn't say,"I have a strategic plan that I think might work."

A North Star

Doug Conant, the former CEO of Campbell Soup, told me the most important thing he did when he became the leader of the company was to share the vision. He said he shared it before every meeting. Whether the meeting was just a few people or hundreds gathered for a sales meeting, he shared the vision: *To build the world's most extraordinary food company by nourishing people's lives everywhere, every day.* He told me that he kept sharing and reinforcing the vision in order to align everyone in the company and point them in the right direction. He didn't stop saying it once he had steered the company away from the brink of bankruptcy and into profitability. He kept sharing the vision over and over again, letting everyone know where they were going and why they were going there.

The vision a positive leader creates and shares serves as a North Star that points and moves everyone in an organization in the right direction. The leader must continually point to this North Star and remind everyone that this is where we are going. Yes, we were here yesterday. Yes, this is what happened in the past. But this is where we are going *now*. We don't have a perfect set of plans because the world is always changing, but we do have a North Star that will guide us. We don't have a perfect road map, but we have a path forward and we have each other. Let's keep our eyes on the North Star and keep moving forward.

Sharing a vision and a North Star is important because everyone needs one. Everyone needs something to hope for and work toward. As humans, we have an innate desire to be great and do something great. We have a longing to improve and create a brighter and better future and, yet, so often fear holds us back. Stress weakens us. Obstacles test our resolve. Adversity makes us want to give up. A leader who shares a vision and a way forward is a dealer in hope, a believer in the impossible, a champion of what's possible, and a coach who guides and inspires a team to keep improving, and keep moving forward.

Positive Leaders Create and Share a Positive Vision

A Telescope and Microscope

As a positive leader you will want to carry a telescope and a microscope with you on your journey. The telescope helps you and your team keep your eyes on your vision, North Star, and big picture. The microscope helps you zoom-focus on the things you must do in the short term to realize the vision in your telescope. If you have only a telescope, then you'll be thinking about your vision all the time and dreaming about the future but not taking the necessary steps to realize it. If you have only a microscope, then you'll be working hard every day but set-backs and challenges will likely frustrate and discourage you because you'll lose sight of the big picture. You need to frequently pull out your telescope to remind yourself and your team where you are going, and you'll need to look through your microscope daily in order to focus on what matters most and follow through on your commitments. Together they will help you take your team and organization where you want to go.

A simple exercise I like to do with leaders at the end of my talks is to have them each write down their big-picture vision for their team and a zoom-focused action they will focus on in order to be a better leader. As a leader, you can do this simple exercise with the members of your team and organization. Simply have each person identify his or her vision and one action they will commit to in order to achieve it.

Dabo Swinney's Vision

I've worked with Dabo Swinney and Clemson football for the past five years. A few years ago, Dabo told me that the day after he was named the interim head coach of the team, midway through the 2008 season, he had an early-morning meeting with the board of trustees. He hadn't slept much the night before and had a lot on his mind. During the meeting, one of the trustees said his vision was that Clemson would create a program that was like other schools that had great academics and great football. Dabo was tired and wanted to say something but he kept telling himself, "Don't say it, don't say it, don't say it." In the end, he couldn't help himself. He responded to the trustee and said, "Sir, I don't mean this disrespectfully but that's not my vision at all. My vision is much bigger than that. My vision is that we will create a program where all the football programs you mentioned want to be like us. That's my vision."

At the time, they most likely thought Dabo was just filled with a lot of positive words, but he had both a telescope and microscope with him on his journey. In 2011, he crystallized his philosophy that *best* would be the Clemson standard. Everything they did on and off the field was about excellence and being their best. Between 2011 and the writing of this book, Clemson has won at least 10 games every year, made it to the College Football Playoff (CFP) National Championship game two years in a row, and won it this year. More importantly, in a *Wall Street Journal* article ranking all the football programs by success on the field and in the classroom, only Clemson and Stanford were featured in the top-right quadrant of the graph, which means they are the two schools with the highest achievement combining both academic and football success. When Dabo showed me the article and the graph, he said it was what he was most proud of. It was his vision from the

Positive Leaders Create and Share a Positive Vision

moment he took the job, and every day he and his coaches and team worked to realize it.

A funny story about this journey is that when Dabo became the head coach, he asked his athletic director at the time for a television for his office to watch game and practice footage. The athletic director told him it wasn't in his budget and they couldn't buy him one. So Dabo went to the store and, with his own money, bought a television, which he still uses to this day. Sure the television screens are much more high tech than they were in 2008, but this television is special to him. While wrapping his arms around it in a joking way, he told me that if he ever leaves Clemson, he's taking that TV with him. Fast forward to 2017: Clemson just built a $55 million football facility with the latest training and recovery technology, nap rooms, a bowling alley, swimming pool, and *all* the televisions Dabo wants. The finest college football facility in the world is a testament to the power of one person's vision.

Dabo, like most big-time college coaches, had a vision of winning a national championship. When I arrived during training camp to speak to the team before the 2015 season, Dabo gave me a t-shirt that said "Dream the Dream" on the front and "15 for 15, January 11, 2016" on the back. I asked him what that meant. He said it was a vision he had when he woke up from a dream. "I had a dream we were going to play in the national championship on January 11 and go for our 15th straight win of the season. The vision is to win all 15 games we play, hence 15 for 15." At the time, I wondered who could be bold enough to put that on a shirt. By the end of the season, I realized the same guy who was bold enough to make those t-shirts was also bold enough to say that he would have a pizza party at the Clemson .

football stadium (nicknamed Death Valley) if the team made it to the college football playoffs. Well, they made it and 30,000 people showed up for the pizza party. At the time, when Dabo said they would have a pizza party, he had no idea how many would show up or how he would feed everyone. But like in the movie *Field of Dreams*, if you build it, they will come. Pizza restaurants from across the state came together to provide all the pizza and it was one amazing party.

If you watched the 2015 National Championship, you know that Clemson lost to Alabama and failed to make Dabo's dream a reality. But after the game I sat in the locker room and watched an incredible display of positive leadership that I will never forget. Dabo told the team that he was so proud of them and that they just didn't make enough plays to beat a team as good as Alabama. He went on to praise his team and all they had accomplished and thanked the seniors for the legacy of excellence they had left. Then he began talking about the coming year and how excited he was for the future. He shared the vision for the returning players and said, "We will be coming back next year." For the next few minutes he pulled out his telescope and shared what the future looked like and all that they were going to do. I was blown away. Here, he and his team had just lost the National Championship, and Dabo was already inspiring his team with a vision for the future. In that moment he taught me that positive leaders, despite the circumstances, obstacles, and set-backs, keep the vision alive and continue to share it to inspire others. Dabo kept the vision alive all season and Clemson made it back to the 2016 National Championship to play Alabama again, but this time they won with a dramatic touchdown with one second left on the clock.

Positive Leaders Create and Share a Positive Vision

Talk about a once-in-a-lifetime moment, a vision realized, a dream achieved!

Keep the Vision Alive

To understand the importance of keeping your vision alive, let's look at marathon runners. The fewest number of people quit a marathon in the first mile. And the second fewest runners quit in the last mile. I would expect a lot to quit in the last mile because, by that point, they have been running the longest and should be the most physically tired. But they don't quit because they are so close to the finish line. They don't quit because they can see the end in sight. They have a vision of where they are going and they keep running towards it. It shows the power of the mind and vision. The body should give up but it doesn't because the mind sees the finish line. The most people quit a marathon in the 20th mile. That is where they are physically tired and mentally drained. They have run far and still have a long way to go. They lose their vision and so they give up. When I speak to companies, schools, and organizations, I encourage the participants to write down when they experience their 20th mile. We all have a 20th mile. Then, I encourage them to write down the words "Keep your vision alive" because if you keep your vision alive, you won't stop. You won't give up. Like Dabo you'll keep moving forward and inspiring your team along the way.

Make the Vision Come Alive

We've been talking about a lot of concepts and ideas, but my goal with this book is not to just share principles and stories and philosophy, but also practical ideas you can implement. In this spirit, one of the simple ways to transform ideas and visions into results is to have a conversation with the people you lead. You may be the leader of 150 people, 1,500 people, or 15,000 people, but for the purpose of this exercise you will do this with your direct reports, and then each person you lead will do this with their direct reports and so on and so on throughout the team and organization. During each conversation, you share the vision and you ask each person to identify what it means to him or her. For the vision to come to life, it must have meaning to us individually. For example, before I spoke to the leaders of Palmetto Health in South Carolina, I interviewed a bunch of people who worked in their hospitals and asked them the vision and what it meant to them. Amazingly, each person was able to recite the vision and tell me specifically how it resonated on an individual level.

After the people on your team identify what the vision means to them, ask them what their personal vision is and how it can help contribute to the bigger vision of the organization. Then ask them how you can help them on their journey. What do they need from you to be their best? Finally, ask them how they would like you to hold them accountable. If you have an open and honest conversation like this with each person you lead and continue to communicate and discuss their personal and organizational visions throughout the year, you'll see the power of a vision come to life. When people know how they are contributing to a bigger vision and have a bigger purpose at work—and feel like their manager-leader-coach genuinely cares about them—the research shows that engagement soars. We will talk more about this later in the book, but for now

Positive Leaders Create and Share a Positive Vision

consider this a great way to share, discuss, and bring the vision to life, one person at a time.

My Vision

I love learning and talking about the power of a vision because it's a vision that has driven me to overcome all the obstacles I have faced to do the work I do now. In 2005 I was on a plane headed to a speaking engagement in Portland, Oregon. I was energized about speaking and thinking about how much the three restaurant franchises I owned were draining me. While reading a magazine, I came across an article that was titled "How to Know When to Sell Your Business," and I thought that maybe it was time to sell the restaurants. On my way home, I read a completely different magazine and came across an article titled "How to Value Your Business When Selling." I didn't think it was a coincidence, so when I walked in the door of my house, I told my wife it was time to sell the restaurants. The signs were clear. I was going to do what I loved and focus 100 percent of my time and energy on writing and speaking. My wife wasn't as excited and optimistic. She asked what would happen if it didn't work out. I was only doing a few speaking engagements a month, didn't have a best-selling book, and we certainly weren't going to get rich from selling the restaurants. We could survive a year or two, but if writing and speaking didn't work out, then what?!?! I told her there were no other options. Somehow, some way, it was going to work out. And it was then that my vision was born. I was going to inspire and empower as many people as possible, one person at a time. Six months after selling the restaurants, I was walking and praying because the writing and speaking weren't going well and I was filled with fear and doubt. That's when the idea for *The Energy Bus* came to me. When I returned home I ran upstairs to my home office and started writing. Three and a half weeks later I had a manuscript that I sent out, which lead to over 30 rejection letters from publishers. The agent I had found told me I should consider giving up on finding a publisher and just self-publish. In those days self-publishing wasn't mainstream like it is now, so that route felt like a letdown.

I thought about giving up, but I couldn't. I had a vision and I kept thinking about it. A few weeks later while sitting in a Barnes and Noble and dreaming about my own book being on the shelf, I saw several books published by John Wiley and Sons and realized we hadn't sent my manuscript to them yet. I asked the agent to send it to them, which she did, and it landed on the desk of Shannon Vargo. Shannon had only been on the job for a few months but she read the manuscript and decided she wanted to publish it. It turns out she had a best friend with a husband named George, the name of the main character, and she also liked the story. I remember getting the call that they were going to publish it. It was truly one of the best moments of my life. The publisher said they wouldn't give me a lot of money for an advance but they could publish it in six months. I was more than excited because I didn't care about the money. I just wanted this book out there so I could live and share my vision.

When the book came out it was surprisingly a huge hit in South Korea. It was a top-ten best seller there, but not one bookstore in the United States would carry it. My vision was being tested. I decided to go on a 28-city tour to share the

Positive Leaders Create and Share a Positive Vision

message about the book and, hopefully, inspire and empower as many people as possible, one person at a time. I mapped out a plan for the tour, drove cross country, and gradually made my way back to Florida, one city at a time. My friend Daniel Decker, who is still my business partner, called up local radio and television stations a few days before I arrived in each city and tried to book me on their shows. We planned a book signing or a talk at a local library or coffee shop in each city. We honestly didn't have an efficient and effective plan, but we did have a lot of hustle and grit. We said I was internationally known, which was true since I was a best seller in South Korea, and, fortunately, I was able to get on a bunch of local television and radio shows, but only a few people showed up to my events. We had five people in one city. Ten people in another city. We had a big crowd of 20 to 30 people in a few cities, and the biggest turnout was about 100 people in Des Moines, Iowa. I believe they showed up because they thought Jeff Gordon, the NASCAR driver, was coming.

The tour wasn't easy. I had two young children at home with my wife and I missed them a lot. I drove thousands of miles through the desert and cornfields and mountains, and got sick along the way in Kansas and Nebraska. Thankfully, Jim Van Allan, my college intern at the time, who is now a great trainer, speaker, and workshop leader for my company, was able to drive *The Energy Bus* and me to a few cities while I slept and recovered. I gave everything I had on that tour and focused on inspiring and empowering anyone who came to see me. The interesting thing was that I met a school principal in one city and that lead to a speaking engagement at a school. I met a businessman and that lead to a speaking engagement at a company. I met a coach and that lead me to speak to my first pro sports team. I didn't have a great plan, but my vision kept me going and it lead to many of the great relationships I have to this day. Ten years later, my vision still keeps me going. It's the reason why I wrote this book, created Positive University, and started The Energy Bus for Schools program, where our mission is to transform the negativity prevalent in education to create positive school cultures and develop positive leaders (both adults and students). I've experienced the power of a vision in my own life and I know what is possible when you see it and act on it. I don't tell you my story so you'll be impressed with me. I tell it so you'll look inside yourself and look out into the world and know that you possess the greatest power in the universe: the power to see a positive future and create it.

Chapter 5

Positive Leaders Lead with Optimism, Positivity, and Belief

The most important characteristic of a leader is optimism.

—Bob Iger, CEO of Disney

The research shows that optimism is a competitive advantage, but we don't need research to tell us what we already know to be true. After all, if you don't believe in your vision and where you are going, and you are not optimistic that you'll get there, you'll be like the many who give up before reaching their goal and dream. They give up because of the struggle, the negativity, the frustration, the adversity, the fear, the rejection, the naysayers, and the circumstances that seem insurmountable. They give up because they don't have the optimism, positivity, and belief to keep moving forward. But you don't have to give up. You don't have to settle for the status quo. You can see a brighter and better future and work to create it. Do you remember me talking about Rick Hendrick in Chapter 3? He is the man who built both the Hendrick Automotive Group into the largest privately owned dealer group in the United States and turned Hendrick Motorsports into the winningest racing organization in the modern era. Well you probably won't be surprised to know that he lists optimism as his number-one key to success; faith comes in second, attitude sixth, and enthusiasm tenth. Optimism, positivity, and belief are the fuel that positive leaders need to keep moving forward and drive results.

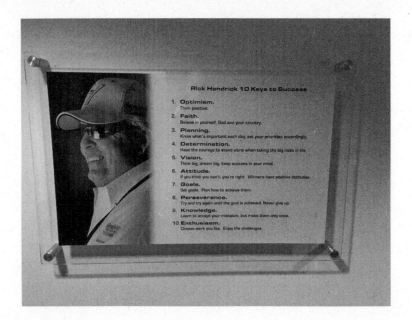

When Donna Orender was the senior VP of strategic development for the PGA Tour, she helped the Tour forge a new path forward, launched new tournaments, developed revenue models that didn't exist yet, implemented ideas and initiatives that had never been done, and exponentially increased television revenue and grew the popularity of the game. How did she do it? The same way she uplifted, transformed, and grew the popularity of professional women's basketball as commissioner of the WNBA. Orender leads with optimism and has a system to build collective belief in her team and organization. When she became the commissioner of the WNBA, there was a lot of negativity amongst the people in the corporate office. There was a feeling that no one cared about women's basketball and a lack of belief that the organization could be successful. But Orender saw the passion and optimism in the coaches and players, and she believed in them and in the future of the WNBA. Orender identified the believers and began building an optimistic belief system around them. Then she showed proof of concept and early successes to the next level of believers and got them to buy in and believe in the WNBA's future. She focused on one success at a time. She said, "You have to give people excuses to say yes. Some will be all in based on what you say. Some you need to show." For those who still didn't believe, she had to help them leave, letting them know they weren't in the right place. Orender said, "I always believe in what's possible. There isn't a problem that can't be solved. There are often multiple answers and you have to find the best one. This isn't Pollyanna positive. You must not only be positive but effective too. You can be positive but not effective. It's about deciding the highest and best use of our energy. Once you decide the way forward, you execute."

It's hard to find someone who exemplified the power of optimism and belief more than Marva Collins. Frustrated by the bureaucracy and inadequate teaching in public education, in 1975 she started her own elementary school, Westside Preparatory School, in Garfield Park, an impoverished Chicago neighborhood. There she taught children, many of whom had been wrongly labeled as "learning disabled," to read, write, and study classical literature. The system said they couldn't learn, but Collins believed that with discipline, structure, hard work, and positive reinforcement they could, and many of her former students say she inspired them to believe as well. She would often put her hand under their chins, lift their heads up, and say, "You are brilliant." One of her students said when you keep hearing that you are brilliant, you start to believe it. The

Positive Leaders Lead with Optimism, Positivity, and Belief

television show *60 Minutes* did a special on Collins and brought a bunch of her former students back for a reunion. Many of those who were told they had learning disabilities were now teachers, attorneys, sales leaders, and successful college graduates. They are living proof of the power of a positive leader who believed in them and was optimistic about their future.

Believe It and You'll See It

People often say they'll believe it when they see it. But in order to see results you have to believe they are possible. William Bratton was the New York City police commissioner under Mayor Rudy Giuliani during the '90s, when the city had a major crime problem. Many said it was a hopeless problem that couldn't be solved, but they solved it. Years later, Bratton was asked how he did it. He said he met individually with the chiefs in each of the five boroughs and asked each one of them the same question, "Do you believe crime can be reduced in your area?" Three of the chiefs said no and two said yes. Bratton said, "Unfortunately, I had to fire three people that day. Why play the game if you don't believe you can win?"

Doug Conant faced a similar challenge when he became the CEO of The Campbell Soup Company. At the time the iconic soup company was likely headed towards bankruptcy or about to be bought by another company. Conant said one of the first things he had to do after evaluating the business and the company was fire 300 of the company's top 350 leaders because these leaders didn't believe Campbell Soup could be turned around. They didn't see or believe in a way forward, so he had to replace them with optimists who would help him transform the company. Together, they focused on their new vision, created a highly engaged workforce and culture, and produced a remarkable turnaround.

If You Don't Have It, You Can't Share It

Please know that I'm not saying as a leader that you should fire all your pessimists. What worked for William Bratton and Doug Conant may not work for everyone. Every situation is different. I'm simply providing examples that demonstrate the importance of a leader's optimism and belief in overcoming challenges and turning around negative, seemingly hopeless situations. The fact is, if you don't have optimism and belief, you can't share it. If you don't have it, you can't transform your team and organization with it. It starts first and foremost with you. Before you look at anyone else on your team and in your organization, look in the mirror and ask yourself: Are you a positive leader? Do you believe? Are you optimistic? Are you feeding others with the positivity they need to succeed? Perhaps you are like me and are not naturally positive. Perhaps you have to work at it. The great news is that you can cultivate it. You can become more positive as a leader. You can feed yourself with positivity so you can share it with others.

Feed the Positive Dog

In my book *The Positive Dog*, Matt and Bubba are two dogs living in a shelter. Matt, who everyone calls Mutt, is really negative. Bubba is a positive dog who teaches Matt an important lesson.

He says that we all have two dogs inside of us. We have a negative dog and a positive dog, and they fight all the time. Matt asks Bubba who wins the fight, to which Bubba replies, "The one you feed the most, so feed the positive dog." I based this story on an ancient fable about two wolves, but whether we are talking about wolves, dogs, or humans, we all have a positive-versus-negative battle going on each day. Every moment and every situation presents to us an opportunity to see and experience the positive or the negative. Each day we can feed the positive dog or the negative dog inside of us, and whichever one we feed, grows. So feed the positive dog.

Talk to Yourself

Dr. James Gills accomplished the remarkable feat of completing a double triathlon (two triathlons back to back with only a 24-hour break). Even more remarkable is that Gills completed a double triathlon six times, and the last time he did it he was 59 years old. When asked how he did it, he gave the best advice I've ever heard. He said, *"I've learned to talk to myself instead of listen to myself."* He memorized scripture and would recite it to himself when he needed a boost. Gills continued, "If I listen to myself, I hear all the reasons why I should give up. I hear that I'm too tired, too old, too weak to make it. But if I talk to myself, I can give myself the encouragement and words I need to hear to keep running and finish the race." It's the same way with life. Too often we listen to ourselves and hear all the complaints, self-doubt, fear, and negativity that lead to unhappiness, failure, and unfulfilled goals. But just because you have a negative thought doesn't mean you have to believe it. Many of your negative thoughts come from fear and the truth is that fear is a liar. I've learned that instead of listening to the negative lies, we can choose to feed ourselves with the positive truth. We can speak truth to the lies and fuel up with words, thoughts, phrases, and beliefs that give us the strength and power to overcome our challenges and create an extraordinary life, career, and team. Whatever comes your way, just keep running, stay positive, talk to yourself (instead of listening to yourself), and make sure you celebrate and raise your hands in the air when you've reached your destination!

It's All How You See It

Another way we feed the positive dog is through our perspectives and how we see the world. For example, while visiting with and speaking to several major league baseball teams during spring training, I kept hearing from players and coaches that baseball is "a game of failure." After all, even a Hall of Fame player will fail to get a hit two out of three times. And most players will fail to get a hit three out of four times. A pitcher will give up hits and home runs; fielders will make errors. Yes, baseball is a game where people fail often. But I saw it differently and, when talking to the teams, I offered a different perspective. I said, "I don't believe baseball is a game of failure. I believe it's a game of opportunity!" No matter what happened on the last play, pitch, or at bat, players get the opportunity to make the next one great. In the words of Babe Ruth, "Every strike brings me closer to the next home run." It's the same way with life. Anyone pursuing anything worthwhile will fail and fail often. I certainly have failed many times, but when I look back I realize I wasn't failing, I was growing. I wasn't failing, I was becoming. I've learned that you can dwell on the past or look forward to making the next opportunity great. You can see life as a game of failure or opportunity. It's all how you see it.

Tell Yourself a Positive Story

When tragic events like 9-11, the Oklahoma City bombing, or the attacks on the Boston Marathon happen, *we have a choice* in the narrative we tell after the event. Terrorists want us to tell stories of fear, despair, and hopelessness. Yet New Yorkers, Oklahomans, and Bostonians decided to tell themselves and the world a very different narrative. They told stories of strength, perseverance, and resolve—courage, faith, unity, and love. This is significant because the stories you tell yourself determine how you respond to adversity and how you live your life. When Charlie Ebersol, a television producer, survived a plane crash that killed his younger brother, one of the first things his mother told him was, "You are allowed to be sad but you can't be mad, sad. You have to have a purpose and turn this into something good." Ebersol said that this perspective changed his life. He went on to sell his company, gave up all the things he had been doing, and focused only on the things he loved—which lead to him producing inspiring television shows and documentaries. In television and life people get knocked down. Those who see themselves as victims stay down. But those who see themselves as heroes get back up and, armed with optimism, courage, and faith, they move forward and take action to create a brighter and better future.

The story we tell ourselves determines the life we live. In one of my favorite books, *A Million Miles in a Thousand Years*, author Donald Miller tells the story of a friend whose teenage daughter was rebelling, doing drugs, and dating the wrong kind of guy. The dad decided he needed to stop yelling at his daughter and instead needed to create a different narrative for her life. He held a family meeting where he shared that they were going to raise money and build an orphanage in Mexico. At first his family thought he had lost his mind but then they all rallied behind the idea. His daughter even got excited about going to Mexico and meeting the kids there and posting pictures on her website. A few months later, when Miller saw his friend again, he learned that everything had changed for the better. His family was living a better story. His daughter broke up with her boyfriend after he told her she was too fat. The dad said, "No girl who plays the role of a hero in her story dates a guy who uses her. She knows who she is. She just forgot for a little while."

Those who study filmmaking know that in every great movie the main character wants to achieve something, but must overcome adversity and conflict in order to get it. And those who study life know it works the same way. Whether you want to start a business, build a winning team, raise great kids, provide safe drinking water in Africa, help the homeless, find a cure for cancer, educate children, or create a more peaceful world, adversity and conflict will be part of your story as you strive to achieve your goal. But when adversity hits, you can choose to tell yourself and the world a positive story and work passionately to create a positive outcome.

Positive Leaders Lead with Optimism, Positivity, and Belief

Challenge or Opportunity

You can tell yourself a positive story by looking at the events in your life as an opportunity instead of a challenge. There was a British study of 500 charmed people who seemed to have it all—wealth, relationships, great careers, and happiness. When the researchers studied these charmed people, they were surprised to find that every one of them had experienced misfortune in their lives. On the outside, it seemed like they had lived perfect lives, but every one of them faced challenges, adversities, and hardships. Yet despite the various challenges, they all shared the same characteristic. They all turned their misfortune into fortune.[9] In the midst of their struggle, they looked for and found an opportunity. As a leader you must remember that events are going to happen. Challenges are going to come your way. Your job is not to get stuck in the mud. Don't sink to a lower level. Keep your head up. Look for the opportunity and the good that is coming your way.

The Gallup Organization did a study where they asked people to name the best and worst event of their lives. They found that there was an 80 percent correlation between the two events. Somehow the worst event of our lives often leads to the best, if we stay positive, stay the course, and keep moving forward.

Shark or Goldfish

As a leader, your perspective is very important because how you see the world and events determines the world you see and how you respond. In my book *The Shark and the Goldfish*, I share how the waves of change are always coming our way and, when the wave hits, we have a choice. We can resist change or we can ride the wave to a successful future. The research shows that people and companies that thrived during the great recession were the ones who embraced the change. Instead of being like goldfish and waiting to be fed like in the good ole days, they embraced the change and looked for opportunities to find more food. The key factor in their success was their perspective, how they saw the change they were experiencing. Those who saw it as a bad thing and resisted it got crushed by the wave. Those who saw it as a good thing and an opportunity rode the wave to a better future. I recently spoke about thriving through change to all the leaders of a company that owns a lot of local news stations. There was a lot of fear and resistance to the change happening and how people are and will consume local news in the future. The leaders now understand that change is coming their way, like it or not, and if they embrace the change and find new business models they will thrive because of it. They are now sharks and ready to take on the waves of change and experience the ocean of possibility.

Think Like a Rookie

Over the years I've spoken to a lot of organizations and leaders that have been infected by what I call the *curse of experience*. This is where they long for the good ole days, complain about the way things are, and are unwilling to change. They have allowed their past experience, good or

Positive Leaders Lead with Optimism, Positivity, and Belief

bad, to affect their present and future. I saw this a lot in real estate companies during the great recession when I was brought in to reenergize them and boost morale. Before my talk, companies often gave out awards to the best producers, and I realized that a lot of rookies were winning the awards. It hit me that many of the veterans with all their great experience were so shaken up by the economy that they had become goldfish instead of sharks. They had allowed fear to paralyze them and circumstances to define them. They were complaining about the economy instead of creating it. They had the curse of experience and the antidote was to get them to think like rookies again. Rookies aren't tainted by rejection, negative assumptions, or past experiences. They bring an idealism, optimism, and passion to their work. They don't focus on what everyone says is impossible. Instead, with wide eyes they believe anything is possible. Rookies put their heads down, work hard, stay positive, live fearlessly, and are naïve enough to be successful. Rookies don't have experience. They don't know about the way things were. They have no knowledge of the good ole days. Instead, rookies create their good ole days right now. Regardless of how much experience you and your fellow leaders have, I want to encourage you to let your experience be a blessing, not a curse. Let your experience provide you with expertise and let your rookie mindset fuel you with optimism and passion. Mentor the rookies because, for all their effort and energy, they do make mistakes. And yet, let them teach you how to see the world through their eyes. *Think like a rookie,* forget the past, and create your good ole days right now.

Defeating Murphy

I'm sure you have heard of Murphy's Law, right? Whatever can go wrong will go wrong—and usually at the worst possible time. Unfortunately, Murphy's Law seems to play out all too often and, when a series of bad things happens, it can lead you to expect more bad things to happen. Instead of hoping for the best, you start to expect the worst and act accordingly. Football coach Gus Bradley, one of the most positive leaders I've ever met, told me about a great way he helps his team deal with negative events (e.g., a crucial interception, penalty, injury, bad weather, etc.) and avoid the victim mindset that can accompany them. Gus tells his team about this fictional guy named Murphy, whom the law is named after. Murphy is a big jerk who wants to ruin their practice, games, and season. He says that Murphy often shows up at the worst possible time. But instead of being scared of Murphy when he shows up they are going to tackle him. They expect to see Murphy, and when they do they have an even greater expectation that they will defeat him. Life is filled with challenging circumstances, but you can rise above them. Life is hard, but you are strong. The struggle is real, but so is your ability to overcome it. As my friend Erwin McManus said, "Greatness is never born from easy circumstances. We can become stronger when the world becomes harder." So when adversity hits, don't run from it. Don't be scared of it. Face it. Take it on and keep moving forward. Murphy is tough, but you are tougher.

Inside Out

A big part of leadership and moving your team forward through challenges and change is to understand that we don't create our

Positive Leaders Lead with Optimism, Positivity, and Belief

world and success outside in. We create it inside out. This means that your circumstances and the events that happen outside you in the world are not meant to define you. You are meant to define your circumstances. The power is not in the circumstance. It's in your state of mind and the love, passion, soul, purpose, and perspective that you lead and create with. Let's take traffic, for example. One day traffic really bothers you. Another day you are listening to a great song or podcast, you're in a great mood, and the traffic doesn't bother you. Is it the circumstance (traffic) or your state of mind that is producing how you feel? If it was the circumstance, your response would be the same, 100 percent of the time. Remember that it's never about the circumstance. It's not the challenge, change, economy, election, adversity, or setback you are facing. It's always your state of mind and your thinking that produces how you feel and respond. When you see that the world has no power over you, you will lead more powerfully in the world.

Distort Reality

You will also lead more powerfully when you realize that you have the power to distort reality. We often think that reality is objective, but when you understand how positive leaders have changed the world throughout history, it becomes clear that a leader can define reality and distort it in a positive way. Before there was an iPhone, iPad, iCloud, or Apple Watch, there was Steve Jobs, a man with vision, positive ideas, and a reality-distortion field. In Walter Isaacson's biography *Steve Jobs*, he describes how Jobs repeatedly convinced Apple employees that they could meet a project deadline that everyone thought was impossible. Time and time again they would tell Steve he was being unrealistic and there was no way they could create software or hardware in the amount of time he was expecting. Jobs's team said he distorted their reality from pessimism (or some would say from realism) to optimism and, time and time again, they accomplished what they had thought was impossible. His belief was contagious and, as a result, Apple became one of the greatest companies on earth. What could your team achieve if you shared your optimism and belief with them and distorted their reality?

Leadership Is a Transfer of Belief

You may have thought that reality is the result of your circumstances, but it's really a result of your thoughts and beliefs. As we have discussed, how you see the world determines the world you see and experience. Leadership is a transfer of belief. What you believe is possible, and the beliefs you share with your team and organization have a big influence on what you create, build, and accomplish. Pete Carroll, the head coach of the Seattle Seahawks, is well known for his positive leadership style. Carroll said, "The world trains people to be pessimistic. One of the most important things I must do here is make sure my players and staff believe that tomorrow will be better than today." In essence, Pete is saying that he must transfer his belief and optimism to his team. He must remind his players of the power that exists inside them to create the world outside them. He must help his players be optimistic and hopeful in a pessimistic negative and fearful world.

Positive Leaders Lead with Optimism, Positivity, and Belief

I saw the same attitude and leadership in Silicon Valley during the great recession. While the rest of the country was going through the downturn, the people who lead and work for the companies in Silicon Valley refused to participate in the recession. They were too busy trying to change the world. They were surrounded by a bubble of optimism. While companies and businesses around the country were fearfully closing their doors and people were losing their jobs and homes, Mark Zuckerberg was attracting millions of friends on Facebook. Jack Dorsey was building and growing Twitter one tweet and 140 characters at a time. Elon Musk was launching the world's first electric sports car and rockets into outer space with Tesla and SpaceX. Larry Page and Sergey Brin were transforming Google from a search engine into a verb and a ubiquitous part of our lives. And hundreds of other innovators and start-ups were changing the way we communicate, connect, learn, read, search, interact, live, and work.

In Silicon Valley there is a bubble of optimism that is filled with a collective belief that anything is possible. If you have a great idea, it gets funded. If you are willing to innovate and work hard, the American Dream is very much alive and available to you. If you believe and you can execute and turn this belief into a reality, you can change the world. The innovators of Silicon Valley are alchemists who turn ideas into gold. Where others see what is impossible, they see what is possible. While others see them as crazy, they see the future. When a new idea or product fails, they come up with a better idea and a better business. Failure is accepted as a part of innovation and growth. Ideas are tested and the best ones win. Silicon Valley embodies the can-do spirit, creativity, drive, and courage that positive leaders embrace to create innovations that change the world. But you don't have to live in the valley to embrace their approach. Amazon and Starbucks have transferred that spirit of belief to Seattle. Zappos has found happiness in Las Vegas. GM, Ford, and the big auto companies are powering forward with new ideas and making world-class cars in Detroit. And thousands of start-ups located in cities and universities around the planet are dreaming of ways to change the world. Every business and leader, wherever they are located, can create a bubble of optimism and transfer their belief to their team, tribe, organization, community, city, and following. There is always a new idea or a better way of doing something waiting for someone to implement it. It can be you!

Lead with Faith Instead of Fear

Ultimately, being a positive leader is all about leading with faith in a world filled with cynicism, negativity, and fear. The ultimate battle we face every day is the battle between faith and fear. As a leader you must realize that your people are facing this battle daily. They are filled with fear, doubt, and uncertainty, and it's your job to inspire them with faith. Leading with optimism, positivity, and belief comes down to leading with faith instead of fear. In the beginning of this book, I shared how positive leaders are the ones who change the world. I shared how the future belongs to those who believe in it and have the belief, resilience, positivity, and optimism to overcome all the challenges in order to create it. But we know that positive leaders don't do it alone. They do it with others, with the team they build and the people they inspire, encourage, and lead with faith on the journey.

A few years after Alan Mulally became the CEO of Ford, the economy went into a tailspin, the great recession hit, and they faced the worst economic climate since the Great Depression. There were many moments where it looked like all the work Mulally, his team, and employees had done to restructure the company, build a united leadership team, create best-of-class automobiles, and become profitable was for naught. At the bottom of the recession when things looked the most bleak the government bailed out Ford's competitors and the rules of the game seemed to change. Mulally told his team, "You have to expect the unexpected and you have to deal with it. Whining is not a plan. Wallowing is not a plan. We have a plan, and if we need to adjust it, we will." Despite his team members' fears, Mulally remained steadfast in his belief in his plan, in his team, and in Ford's future. Where others might have waffled and crumbled from fear, Mulally was an optimist who continued to share his belief with his team and company. When the economy finally turned around, his optimism, faith, and plan produced exponential growth and profits for Ford. Without his leadership, this wouldn't have happened.

Be an Over-Believer

Dabo Swinney was asked recently if he considered himself an overachiever for all the success he has generated at Clemson. He responded, "I'm not an overachiever. I'm an over-believer." When Dabo became the head coach of Clemson, he put a sign in the team meeting room that said "Believe" because he knew there wasn't a lot of belief—either inside or outside the program—that they could be great. Clemson was known for losing games they should win. It happened to them so often, people called it "Clemsoning." So the man who had never been a head coach or coordinator, whose father left when he was young, who was homeless for a time growing up, who had left coaching for a few years to pursue a career in real estate, who had believed in himself enough to become a walk-on at Alabama and had come to believe that anything was possible knew his number-one priority was to inspire his team to believe—and he did. Dabo is so full of genuine belief and faith that he shares it with everyone around him. He believes in his players more than they believe in themselves. He believes in them so much that their belief in themselves rises. Most of all I've noticed that, regardless of the circumstance, no matter the challenge, whatever the setback, he never stops believing and sharing his belief with his team. On January 9, 2017, I was in the locker room with the team at halftime of the National Championship game. Clemson was trailing 14–7. Dabo told his team, "Somehow, someway, we are going to win this game, guys. I don't know how, but we are going to win." The guys may have been fearful but Dabo instilled them with faith. It was something he had done every day since 2008. With every setback and failure over the years, Dabo would say, "God doesn't say oops. God doesn't make mistakes. There is a bigger plan. Trust in it." Dabo told me he was constantly inspired by Galatians 6:9, "Let us not become weary in doing good for at the proper time we will reap a harvest if we do not give up." He led with faith and his team acted with fearlessness and reaped a harvest at the proper time.

Don't Stop Believing

Great teams are collectively positive. They have a collective belief and contagious optimism—and it starts with you. When you believe, you can inspire others to believe. When you have faith, you can inspire others with it. You will face a lot of adversity, resistance, and negativity, but always remember that your certainty, optimism, belief, and faith must be greater than all the negativity, fear, and doubt. Share your optimism, belief, and faith with your team. Show them the way forward. Point them toward your North Star. Explain where you are going and why you are going there. Talk about the challenges but explain why you can overcome them. Transfer your belief to them. Feed them with positivity. Speak life into them. Believe in them when they don't believe in themselves. Lift them up when they are down. Inspire them to do more, give more, and become more than they ever thought possible. Tell them that fear and faith have one thing in common. They both believe in a future that hasn't happened yet. Fear believes in a negative future. Faith believes in a positive future. If neither has happened yet, why wouldn't we choose to believe in a positive future? Why wouldn't we choose to believe our best days are ahead of us, not behind us. Tell your team that if you believe your best days are behind you, they are. If you believe your best days are ahead of you, they are. What we believe matters, so let's believe, work hard, and make it happen.

Even after Clemson won the National Championship, Dabo told the team in the locker room, "You are National Champions now, but I want you to be champions in life too. Be great husbands and fathers. This won't be the best thing to happen in your life. God has even more in store for you. The best is yet to come." They had just reached the peak of success as a team and Dabo was talking about their future as men. In essence, he was saying whether you win or lose, don't stop believing. That's leadership.

Your Leadership Journey

I don't know where you are on your leadership journey. I know that I wasn't always positive and I've become a more positive leader over the years. Perhaps you are already very optimistic and positive. Or maybe you've been a pessimist or someone who says, "I'm just being realistic." Hopefully you understand that leadership is not just about what you do but what you can inspire, encourage, and empower others to do. Regardless of your circumstances and challenges, there is a future waiting to be created and, with your leadership, optimism, belief, and faith, your team and organization will be the one to create it. On your leadership journey, it will take all your optimism, belief, and positivity to help others become all that they are meant to be. It will also require your ability to develop relationships with them, which we will discuss later in the book. But if you start the process by building a positive culture, sharing the vision, feeding yourself with positivity, creating your own reality-distortion field, and leading with optimism, you and your team will be well on your way to creating a positive future.

Positive Leaders Lead with Optimism, Positivity, and Belief

Chapter 6

Positive Leaders Confront, Transform, and Remove Negativity

Being positive won't guarantee you'll succeed but being negative will guarantee you won't.

P ositive leadership is not just about feeding the positive, but also about weeding out the negative. As a leader you must recognize that negativity exists and you can't ignore it. One of the biggest mistakes leaders make is that they ignore the negativity within their team and organization. They allow it to breed and grow, and it eventually sabotages the team and organization. You must address the negativity. Confront it, transform it, or remove it.

I remember getting a call in 2007, shortly after *The Energy Bus* was published, from Jack Del Rio, who was the head coach of the Jacksonville Jaguars at the time. A friend had given him the book; he read it, and called to ask if I would meet with him. Keep in mind that I had just written the book. It wasn't in U.S. bookstores yet, although it was big in South Korea. I had never worked with a sports team before, never mind a professional sports team, and never spoken to a leader of his stature before. Now, as I sat across from him he told me that he was allowing energy vampires to get to him and the book helped him realize that he needed to deal with the negativity. It also reminded him to be more positive than the negativity he was facing. He asked me to speak to the team, and for some reason I boldly said I would if he gave the players a copy of the book. He agreed, and as I drove home it was confirmation that everyone, even legendary football players, great coaches, and world-class leaders deal with the same negativity that we all need to overcome. Thankfully, I had written something that would help them. Looking back, I believe the reason why *The Energy Bus* has been read by so many leaders and teams is because it addresses the negativity every team, organization, and leader will face. It was a lesson I had learned in my own life before I wrote the book.

Your Positivity Must Be Greater than All the Negativity

I remember telling my dad that I was going to be a writer and speaker, that I had found my calling. His response was, "What the heck do you want to do that for? That won't amount to anything. That's a load of junk. Just focus on your restaurants." He used other words I can't print. At the time, I still owned a few restaurant franchises and my father thought I should just focus on that. A restaurant was practical. Writing and speaking was just a fantasy. A few years after my dad gave me his "encouraging" advice, I appeared on the *Today Show*. The episode was called "Get Energized Today." It was my first time on national television and I was terrified. I coached several people on the show about having more energy and optimism for their life and work and, as I walked out of the studio, my dad called me on the phone. He said, "Your mother and I just saw you on television. You really made a difference. We are so proud of you. We always knew you could do it." I knew my dad didn't remember being negative in the past and I realized in that moment that every one of us will deal with negativity and naysayers on our journey. Not everyone will have the same vision as you. Not everyone will believe in your dreams. Not everyone will get on your bus. But to succeed, your positive energy must be greater than all the negativity.

Gandhi said, "I will not let anyone walk through my mind with their dirty feet," and neither should you. You may have a negative team. You may have negative customers, patients, neighbors, or parents. The first rule of thumb when weeding the negative is to not let it bring you down. Be more positive than the negativity you face. Don't be afraid of it. Negativity is like a barking dog. It seems powerful, but when you look right in its eyes, it runs away. Negativity is no match for your courage and positivity. I know because I've worked with many positive leaders and watched how they have confronted, transformed, and removed the negativity and achieved amazing results.

No Energy Vampires Allowed

In 2011 Mark Richt, the head football coach of the University of Georgia at the time, had his team read *The Energy Bus* and invited me to speak to the team. I spoke before the season and, unfortunately, they lost their first two games. Georgia had been underperforming during the previous few seasons and the media was reporting that Richt was on the hot seat and would lose his job if this season didn't go well. I texted him after the second loss and said "I am sorry I didn't help more. I believe in this team. I believe you all are going to turn it around." Richt texted me back and said, "Jon, the guys are still on the bus. In years past we've allowed energy vampires to ruin this team but

Positive Leaders Confront, Transform, and Remove Negativity

not this year. This year we won't allow it." In the team meeting room, Richt had an artist draw a large picture of an energy vampire on the wall facing the seats where the players sit. If a player or coach acted like an energy vampire, the team took his picture from the media guide and put it on the wall. No one wanted to be on the wall. It was a message from Richt to his team that they would stay positive through their adversity and challenges. It worked, and the team went on to win the next 10 games in a row and made it to the SEC Championship.

Why Wait?

I shared this story with the University of Tennessee football team a few years after working with UGA and, when I was finished speaking, coach Butch Jones told the team the meeting was over but then called out the names of 10 guys and told them to stay. I asked Butch who these guys were and he said, "Oh, these are our energy vampires." I said, "Oh, you are going to deal with that now?" He said, "Yes. Why wait?" After the meeting, Butch walked out of the room and into the hallway where I was speaking to the athletic director. I asked him how it went. He said, "Powerful. Most of the guys admitted they were being energy vampires and have committed to being a positive influence on our team. They are going to be difference makers for us this season. But a few of the guys don't get it, won't change, and we will have to let them off the bus." Tennessee overcame a lot of adversity that season and made their first bowl game in years. They were a great example how a team that stays positive together wins together. I'll never forget Butch's words: "Why wait?" To build a winning team you must create a positive culture where negativity can't breed and grow, and the sooner you start confronting, transforming, weeding, and removing it from your team, the stronger and more positively contagious your culture and team will be.

The First Step Is to Transform

The first step in dealing with an energy vampire on your team is not to remove but to transform. No one really wants to be an energy vampire. These people are likely negative for a reason. The first steps should always be to listen with empathy and love, and try to understand and transform. For example, Martin, a leader with the company Seventh Generation, told me that he put a sign on his door that said *Energy vampires welcome. Expect to be transformed.* He had a lot of great conversations and was able to transform a lot of negative energy into positive results.

Richt also had a number of his players come to his office and tell him they weren't going to be energy vampires anymore. Several of the players from that team are thriving in the NFL. Several have become successful businessmen and it's rewarding to hear how the experience was a defining moment for a bunch of them. Mark didn't just kick them off the bus. He confronted the negativity, invited them onto the bus, sought to transform them—and it worked.

Start at the Culture Level

I have found that the best way to deal with energy vampires in your organization is at the culture level, where you set the expectation that people who drain the energy of others will not

Positive Leaders Confront, Transform, and Remove Negativity

be tolerated. You talk about the negative impact of negativity. You explain that one person can't make a team but one person can break a team. You talk about what a great culture looks like and how you want everyone to be a positive contributor to it. You make it clear what a great team looks like, and it doesn't look like a bunch of energy vampires. By putting the energy vampires' pictures on the wall, Richt was in essence telling his team, "We will not allow negativity to sabotage our team and goals." Shawn Eichhorst did the same thing by putting a "No energy vampires allowed" sign above his office door when he became the new athletic director at Nebraska. He wasn't shunning people, but rather letting them know he was building a positive culture and wouldn't allow negativity to sabotage their university and athletic programs. He faced a barrage of negativity in his early years but slowly and steadily built his culture with a positive, principles-based approach and transformed many hearts and minds along the way. I've worked with Eichhorst and Nebraska Athletics for five years and have witnessed the effectiveness of his approach. I've also heard from a number of school principals and business leaders who have addressed negativity at the culture level as well. While they didn't utilize Richt's strategy of putting energy vampires' pictures on the wall (I think they made the right choice, by the way), they made it clear in staff meetings, book discussions, and viewings of some of our videos, that negativity drains others and sabotages team performance. It is not acceptable. This works wonders for most people in an organization. When you feed the positive and create a culture where energy vampires are uncomfortable being negative, they will either change or walk off the bus themselves. Whether they stay and become positive or leave and stay negative, you will have improved your culture and moved your team in the right direction.

Remove the Negativity

But what if the energy vampires don't leave? What if they remain energy vampires and stay on the bus? I see this all the time. Not everyone is willing to change. No matter how much you try to help someone transform and grow there will be some who are negative no matter what you do. I heard from a school principal who invited all of her staff on the Energy Bus. She shared her vision for the road ahead and asked who was all in. All but two teachers bought in. She did everything she could to get those two teachers to be positive contributors. She documented and documented and documented, which you have to do for legal and personnel reasons, and eventually she had to let them off the bus. She told me that now they are on another bus somewhere else and her staff is feeling more positive and energized than ever. Two negative teachers were infecting their culture and mission to impact the lives of children. But since they were removed, the culture, morale, and energy has improved dramatically. If transforming the negativity doesn't work, you must remove it. Your job as a leader is to create an environment where your people can do their best work without being affected by an energy vampire. You have to feed and weed, weed and feed.

Sooner or Later

I'm often asked how soon an energy vampire should be removed. How soon is too soon or how late is too late? I can't

Positive Leaders Confront, Transform, and Remove Negativity

give you a definitive answer. Every situation is different. When I owned a few restaurants, I definitely kept a few energy vampires on my team longer than I should have. I had one manager at a store that wasn't doing very well. Sales kept dropping and since it was the location furthest from my home, I spent the least amount of time there. I decided to sell that location to a friend and former manager who lived in the area and wanted to open his own place. I had a meeting with the negative manager to let him know what was going on and to reassure him that I had found him another job managing another franchise owned by the other franchisee in town. I wanted to make sure he was taken care of. I'll never forget what he said to me. "You know, Jon, I think I'm going to use this opportunity to get out of the restaurant business because I hate this f—in' job. I smile at the customers like you ask me to, but I hate every single one of them." I sure didn't do a good job of hiring a positive leader for that location and, looking back, I knew he wasn't a good manager, but I honestly have trouble letting people go. If I could do it again I would have let him go sooner. Yet, there were also times I kept people I probably shouldn't have and eventually helped them transform. That's why there's no perfect answer here, but it's something you should continue to evaluate and think about as you lead your team and organization and deal with energy vampires.

One other note on this topic: Even if you let someone off the bus, it doesn't mean you have to let them out of your life. I tell college coaches all the time that even if you have to remove a player from the team, you should still try to invest in that player to help him transform and turn his life around. You may have to let people go for a variety of reasons, because they are hurting the team, but you can still find ways to invest in them and help them grow.

Lead from Where You Are

One of the most frequent types of emails I receive come from people who tell me they are emerging leaders in an organization but, since they don't have the power to hire and fire, they want to know what they should do with the energy vampires they work or interact with at work. I tell them the same thing I wrote in the beginning of this chapter. The first rule is to be more positive than the negativity you face. Become a positive force of positive energy that demonstrates to others what real positivity in the form of love, patience, kindness, and care looks like. Lead by example and lead from where you are. Look at every energy vampire as an opportunity to strengthen your positivity. I try to do this with my teenagers and it has made me a much better leader. We are all on a leadership journey and the first step in becoming a better leader is becoming a better you. Learning to stay positive when surrounded by negativity is a great training ground and, as you develop your own positivity and ability to deal with energy vampires, you will grow as a person and leader. You may not be driving the big bus and deciding who is on it, but you can make your bus great and let it serve as a model for other leaders and people in the organization.

Implement the No Complaining Rule

I didn't invent the rule. I discovered it while having lunch with Dwight Cooper, a tall, thin, mild-mannered former basketball

79

player and coach who had spent the last 15 years building and growing a company he co-founded into one of the leading nurse staffing companies in the world. Cooper's company, PPR, had been named one of *Inc.* magazine's "Fastest-Growing Companies" several times, but on the day we met, it had been named one of the best companies to work for in the country, and Cooper was sharing a few reasons why. Cooper told me about the no complaining rule. He said he had read *The Energy Bus* and realized that, while energy vampires can sabotage your business and team, so can subtle negativity in the form of complaining.

Cooper compared energy vampires to a kind of topical skin cancer. They don't hide. They stand right in front of you and say, "Here I am." As a result, you can easily and quickly remove them. Far more dangerous is the kind of cancer that is subtle and inside your body. It grows hidden beneath the surface, sometimes slow, sometimes fast, but either way, if it's not caught, it eventually spreads to the point where it can and will destroy the body. Complaining is this kind of cancer to an organization, and Cooper had seen it ruin far too many good companies. He was determined not to become another statistic, and *the no complaining rule* was born.

The rule is simple: *You are not allowed to complain unless you also offer one or two possible solutions.* Cooper said, "We introduced the rule to everyone in the company and now share it during interviews with people who want to join our team. We let them know that if you are a complainer this isn't the right place for you. If you want to focus on solving problems, then we would love to have you and will surely listen to you."

I knew Cooper's idea was brilliant. The no complaining rule was a great way to weed out the energy vampires and turn negative energy into positive solutions. I had to share it with others, so I wrote a book called *The No Complaining Rule* to spread the idea. I explained that the goal of the no complaining rule is not to eliminate all complaining. It aims to stop the mindless, chronic complaining that fosters negativity and doesn't help anyone. And the bigger goal is to turn justified complaints into positive solutions. After all, every complaint represents an opportunity to turn something negative into a positive. We can utilize customer complaints to improve our service. Employee complaints can serve as catalysts for innovation and new processes. Our own complaints can serve as signals that let us know what we don't want so we can focus on what we do want. And most importantly, we can *use the no complaining rule* to develop a positive culture at work.

Does it work? You bet. In a commoditized market, Cooper's company is outperforming the competition by leaps and bounds. Like Cooper, with one simple rule, you can prevent the spread of toxic negative energy and empower your team to improve, innovate, and grow. I've heard from hundreds of companies, schools, and teams that have transformed their culture and team dynamic with it. But it doesn't happen without positive leadership. As a leader, it starts with you. If you are complaining, you're not leading. If you are complaining, you are not showing your team the way forward. Complaining causes you and your team to focus on everything but being your best. It causes you to be stuck where you are instead of moving forward to where you want to be. In dysfunctional negative cultures, leaders focus on the problems. In positive,

Positive Leaders Confront, Transform, and Remove Negativity

high-performing cultures, leaders focus on solving problems. Positive leaders show the way forward. They help their team focus on solutions instead of complaints. When a team focuses on solutions instead of complaints, performance rises to a higher level.

Michael Phelps's Positive Leadership

Michael Phelps was recently interviewed by Bob Costas and he described his approach to building a positive team before the 2016 Olympics in Rio.

> Every now and then you hear a bunch of negative comments or someone complaining, and, during training camp, at one of the meetings, I said to the guys that we are getting ready to go to the Olympics. This is what we have to do, and if there is a negative comment, keep it to yourself. The more positivity we have as a team, the better off we are going to be. As soon as I said that, we all became closer and then we really started getting going.

When I heard Phelps say these words, I was thrilled because, in just a few sentences, he defined the essence of positive leadership and shared with the world a truth that I have witnessed countless times over the years. A team with talent can be good, but they must come together to be great. Positivity is the glue that enhances team connection and performance, and it impacts office teams, school teams, church teams, and hospital teams as much as it does Olympic teams. Many people think that you have to choose between positivity and winning, but the truth is you don't have to choose. Positivity leads to winning. That's why feeding the positive and weeding out the negative is essential.

I've seen very positive teams with average talent accomplish more than anyone thought possible. I've also seen negative teams with a lot of talent accomplish far less than everyone thought was possible. Positive teams work together more effectively. They stay positive, connected, and committed through challenges. They maximize each other's talent. They believe together and achieve more together. Positive, high-performing teams don't happen by accident. They are built by positive leaders and team members who weed the negative and feed the positive. When you subtract negativity and add positivity to your talent, the sky is the limit. The great news is that you don't have to be an Olympic champion with 28 medals to begin the process. You can be just like you and me. You can say, "Enough with the negativity. Let's get positive. Let's get going."

Don't Be Negative about Negativity

I would be remiss if I didn't share one final thought about weeding negativity from your team and organization. I must address a misunderstanding that I hear about from time to time and it's one of my motivations in writing this book. Some leaders read *The Energy Bus* and make the mistake of confronting their employees by saying, "You are either on my bus or you are off it." They label anyone who disagrees with them an energy vampire. Instead of inviting people onto the bus, they run them over with it. One of the saddest kinds of emails I receive says something like, "Hey Jon, our bosses gave us *The*

Positive Leaders Confront, Transform, and Remove Negativity

Energy Bus to read, but they are the ones who are energy vampires. I'm trying to be positive but what should I do?" It saddens me to read these emails because it was never my intention for leaders to be negative about negativity. You have to confront it, but you must do so in a positive way. Even more importantly, you must model it. As we will discuss in the next two chapters, positive leadership is also about developing relationships and being the kind of a leader people want to follow. You can't be an energy vampire and be a great leader. You can't be negative and build a positive, high-performing team. You may be dealing with a lot of negativity but you can't lift others up if you lower yourself. You can't help others be positive by being negative. You're the leader, and to be your best and bring out the best in others, you must be a positive leader.

When you feed the positive and weed the negative, you create an environment where you can do your best work as a leader. You can do what the truly great leaders do, and that's build unified and connected teams and great relationships.

Chapter 7

Positive Leaders Create United and Connected Teams

It's the leader's ability to unite and connect people that truly creates great teams and organizations.

P ositive leaders unite instead of divide. They are able to get everyone on the bus and moving in the right direction. They are able to create *unity*, which is the difference between a great team and an average or dysfunctional team. The more united and connected a team and organization is, the more they are able to accomplish together. A vision and North Star are important to point people in the right direction, but it's the leader's ability to unite and connect people that truly creates great teams and organizations. When Alan Mulally took over as the CEO of Ford, he learned that they were regionalized and acted like they were a number of different companies instead of one company. Mulally created a One Ford plan to unite everyone in the company and come together as one team working on one plan to achieve one goal. He created an entire plan and management system designed to have everyone work together as one united and connected team. He held meetings every Thursday at 7AM, where every leader from every division in the company would come together, review the business plan (he called it a BPR—Business Plan Review meeting), and work together to achieve it. He fostered trust, generated transparency and honesty, simplified the business model, brought clarity to their mission and purpose, and, through what many people say is one of the most inspiring and amazing displays of leadership in history, he transformed Ford into one team that accomplished what many of the naysayers and critics thought was impossible. Mulally proved that over time the naysayers are proven wrong and a positive leader who unites others and creates a connected team that works together is proven right.

Connection Is the Difference

The more I have worked with teams and organizations over the years, the more I realize that connection is the *key* to becoming a great organization. Just as Alan Mulally created One Ford by connecting everyone in the company, a leader must work to create a connected team. It starts at the top. A team and organization that's not connected at the top crumbles at the bottom. Therefore, first and foremost, it's important for the leadership team to be connected. I've worked with far too many sports teams and organizations where the leadership teams are not connected. I can literally predict the success of a sports team based on how connected the owner, general manager, and head coach are. I can tell how well a business will weather their challenges and grow by how unified and connected the leaders are. I recently spoke at a meeting where two companies were merging together and leaders from both companies were now becoming one management group. We talked a lot about connecting and did some connection exercises, and you could see and feel the energetic walls break down. Everyone who left the meeting felt that they would be much stronger going forward. Instead of two teams, they were now one team. I knew they were on their way to success because unity and connection are the difference. I once sat in on a morning meeting of the leaders at Mercy Hospital in St. Louis. They were one of the most connected leadership teams I've ever witnessed. It was so powerful you could feel the connection. I was blown away. It was no surprise that their hospital was performing at a very high level.

As a leader, you not only want to be part of a connected leadership team but you also want to make sure you are connecting with everyone in your organization. A lack of connection between leaders and their team leads to a lack of commitment, below-average teamwork, and sub-par performance and results. You can be the smartest person in the room but if you fail to connect with others you will fail as a leader. When you make time to connect with your team and create unity by bringing people together, performance will rise to create a united and connected organization. It's also essential as a leader to enhance the connection between the people on the team and in the organization. As a positive leader, you must be a unifier and connector who fosters relationships between others. One of the biggest complaints I receive from college and pro coaches is that their teams aren't connected. They have a bunch of young men or women who usually focus on themselves, their personal goals, their social media followings, and their egos. They usually have family and friends telling them they should be playing more, scoring more, or getting more recognition. The message they receive from the world is that it's all about the individual, not the team. It's about me, not we. Unfortunately, this may sound like your office and organization as well. There are a lot of silos, personal agendas,

Positive Leaders Create United and Connected Teams

and office politics in the business world. This is also very common in schools, where teachers will say they just care about their classroom and couldn't care less about what's happening in the rest of the building. The disease of *me* infects everyone, not just college athletes. Narcissism and self-focus creates a disconnect between personal goals and team goals, and it undermines the team. People who put themselves and their projects before the team don't build great organizations. People who focus more on their fiefdoms instead of on the kingdom are the ones who blame others when the castle falls. Through my work with coaches and teams, I have found that when coaches and players focus on becoming a connected team, the *me* dissolves into *we*. The individual silos come crumbling down, bonds are strengthened, relationships are developed, and the team becomes much more connected, committed, and stronger. As a leader, you can't allow people to stay isolated. You can't allow the disease of *me* to infect your organization. In my work with schools, I find that many teachers only care about their own classrooms and not about the entire school because the leader hasn't done a great job of connecting the staff and has failed to create a unified school. It's important to create unity and wholeness. It needs to be a priority and it doesn't happen without intentionality and action.

While visiting an NBA team a few years ago, I watched their game the night before I was speaking to the coaching staff. While meeting with the coaching staff, they asked me what I saw. I told them I could tell there was a disconnect between some of the players. They couldn't believe it. They thought one of the coaches had told me what was happening behind the scenes but I didn't need anyone to tell me. When you work with enough teams and organizations you can tell who is connected and who isn't. You know when you see it and you know when you don't. When I don't see solid connections, I try to help nurture them. One of my favorite exercises to help team members become more connected is to have each person share a defining moment in their life. When you learn someone's defining moment, you get to know them a whole lot better and develop a stronger connection with them. My other favorite exercise is to have each person on the team share their hero, hardship, and highlight.

Team Beats Talent When Talent Isn't a Team

One of the reasons why being united is so important is because the more connected you are, the more committed you become. You won't have commitment without connection. Team connection makes a difference. Before the 2013–14 college basketball season, I received a call from Billy Donovan, who at the time was the University of Florida basketball coach. (Now he is the head coach of the Oklahoma City Thunder.) Billy shared the challenges his team was facing and asked for my advice. I shared a few of my ideas with him and he immediately zoomed in on the concept of connection. He said, "That's it, Jon. We often get to the Elite Eight but have trouble pushing through to the Final Four because we aren't as connected as we need to be. If we are more connected, we will have a better chance of winning the tight, big games." Billy and I kept in touch during the season and I was blown away by all he did to connect with his players and foster relationships between them. I never saw a coach do more to invest in a team than what Billy did that season. The walls came crumbling down and, instead of a group of individuals, the Florida team became a connected family. They pushed through the Elite Eight to the Final Four and beat a very talented Kentucky team three times that season. Despite the fact that not one person on their team was drafted into the NBA, Florida was able to beat teams with more talent because they were more connected. They are a great example that team beats talent when talent isn't a team. You may not have the most talented people on your team, but if you are a connected team, you will outperform many talented teams who lack a close bond. When a leader and team connect with each other, commitment, teamwork, chemistry, and performance improve dramatically. Since that time I've worked with a number of coaches to help them build connected teams and I've witnessed the power of connection and unity. Erik Spoelstra, the coach of the Miami Heat, told me he used to spend a majority of his time studying film in the off season. Now he spends more time building connections and team unity than he does watching film. I spoke to his team about the importance of being connected and, over the course of the season, you could see the way they grew to play for each other rather than themselves. It doesn't happen by accident. Erik is an incredible leader and he and his staff are very intentional in finding ways, such as a mandatory Super Bowl viewing party, meaningful team conversations, and intense player development, to consistently connect individually and collectively. Even a coach that has won 1,000 games, Tara VanDerveer, the women's basketball coach at Stanford, is always looking for ways help her team become more connected. We've had great conversations one on one and with her team about fostering connections, and I have loved watching a great leader like her find new ways to connect with her team and help them connect with each other.

Dabo Swinney's Safe Seat

It's not just Dabo Swinney's vision and belief that helped Clemson make it to back-to-back National Championship games and win a title. While I was sitting in Dabo's office in early August, he told me about a chair his friend found and brought him from a remote fishing village. He said it was one of those fishing villages where guys sit around in a circle on these stools and talk about life, family, fishing, and so on. It gave Dabo an idea, and he called it the *Safe Seat*. He placed the stool in the team meeting room and after each practice a different teammate sat on the Safe Seat while the team gathered around him in a circle. Dabo then asked the teammate questions about his life, his heroes, his defining moment, and his challenges. When Dabo was finished asking questions, the rest of the team was free to ask questions. The stool was called the Safe Seat because it was a safe place for each person to share his story and heart with his team. It was a safe place to be vulnerable, knowing that whatever was shared while sitting on the stool would not leave the room. It was a safe spot in a safe room. As each teammate took their turn in the Safe Seat, the players began to know each other a whole lot better. The walls of ego, pride, and selfishness came crumbling down as vulnerability and authenticity paved the way for meaningful relationships, trust, and strong bonds that helped create a connected and committed team. Becoming a connected and committed team helped make the vision and belief come to fruition.

Collaborate and Facilitate

The old dictatorial style of leadership no longer works. Telling people to do it "because I said so" doesn't engage, connect, and unite people. The great leaders of today lead by collaborating and facilitating. Alan Mulally didn't just talk about One Ford, he collaborated with his leaders and everyone in the company to create it. He didn't dominate discussions and conversations during their weekly leadership BPR meetings, but rather guided the conversations and facilitated the process of discussing the issues, challenges, and initiatives that needed to be addressed and implemented and then empowered the other leaders in the room to identify solutions and collaborate in solving them. Great leaders like Mulally don't pretend to know all the answers. They collaborate with others and facilitate the process of finding and implementing the answers. Positive leaders don't succeed on their own. They succeed by getting people to work together. This generates more connection, ownership, and buy-in.

It's important to note that, as a leader, it's not always easy to facilitate and collaborate. You may see where you want to go and become frustrated at first that people don't see the vision and aren't buying in. This could lead to you running ahead with or without your people, hoping they will catch up. But if you don't take your team with you, you'll be ahead of the pack all by yourself. At that point you are just a runner, not a leader, because a leader runs and walks WITH their team.

When I recently visited Penn State to speak to all the athletes and coaches, I sat down with the athletic director, Sandy Barbour, and learned that, to her, the call that "We are

Penn State" is not just a slogan, but also words she lives by as a leader. The word *we* is very important to her and it's why she's the perfect leader to guide her athletic program through all the challenges of the past and the changing landscape of college sports. Various coaches and leaders I met on campus told me privately that "Sandy doesn't talk at us, she walks with us. She works with us. She is there for us. She collaborates with us." Like Alan Mulally, Barbour has a great idea where she wants to go, but she knows that a great team will achieve much more by working together than one person can by working alone.

Don't Let Your Reptile Eat Your Positive Dog

If unity and connection are so essential, then I must address why so many teams and organizations aren't more united and why more leaders don't create unity and connection. I'm convinced that besides selfishness, the enemies are busyness and stress. The research shows when we are busy and stressed, we activate the reptilian part of our brain, which is associated with fear and survival.[10] If you know anything about a reptile, you know that they will never love you. Reptiles are incapable of love because they are all about survival. They're not interested in uniting and connecting with you unless they can eat you. When we are busy and stressed, we activate our reptile brains and are simply about survival. We are not thinking about uniting our teams and connecting with others. We are only thinking of our own survival and how we can get through the day. As a result, we focus on what is urgent rather than what matters. We focus on our to-do list and how to survive rather than on our people and ways to thrive. We don't make the time

Positive Leaders Create United and Connected Teams

to unite and connect. There's actually a scientific term for this: *cortical inhibition*. That is when the amygdala (reptile brain) highjacks the neocortex, the part of the brain where you rationalize, make decisions, pray, practice gratitude, and love. I call the neocortex the *positive dog* part of the brain because of the loving nature of dogs. When you are busy and stressed, your reptile, in essence, eats your positive dog. This is what happened to you anytime you said something you wished you hadn't said. Your reptile ate your positive dog and just blurted out something mean that you would never say if you were thinking clearly. It's what happens to coaches when the TV camera is on them and they are going crazy, yelling at a referee. It's what happens during road-rage incidents. And it's what happens when leaders fail to make time to connect with and unite their teams. The good news is that the research shows we have a quarter-second to override the reptile with our positive dog. We don't have to let the reptile win. We can understand that the enemies are busyness and stress, and recognize when our reptile is coming alive like Bruce Banner does when the Hulk begins to emerge. We can take a deep breath when we realize we are getting stressed and find something to be thankful for in that moment. The research shows you can't be stressed and thankful at the same time. And in each of these moments we can remember that our job as leaders is to unite and connect, and not let the enemies conquer and divide. We can slow down and be more intentional in focusing on the relationships that truly build unity, connection, and great teams. When you know unity is the key and busyness and stress are the enemies, you will slow down and make the time to develop and build great relationships. A united organization happens when you have great relationships. A strong and united culture is created by strong relationships and strong teams. It doesn't happen right away. It requires a lot of patience and a tremendous amount of effort to build unity through great relationships and teamwork. It is created through a lot of love, communication, encouragement, interpersonal connection, commitment, serving, and caring, and it starts with a leader who is someone people want to follow. So now let's talk about how to create unity by building great relationships and teams.

Chapter 8

Positive Leaders Build Great Relationships and Teams

Leadership comes down to taking care of the people in your organization and making them the best they can be, not giving up on them and never failing to be there for them.

Pete Carroll

The first step in uniting people and being a leader is not saying, "Follow me." It's being someone your team wants to follow. You can have the greatest vision and mission statement in the world and be optimistic and positive, but if you are not someone people want to follow, they are not getting on your bus. People follow the leader first and their vision second. What you say is important, but who you are is even more important. Leading is more than sharing a vision and being optimistic. It's more than talking and thinking. It's also about investing in relationships, bringing out the best in others, coaching, encouraging, serving, caring, and being someone that your team can trust. The two questions that the people you lead are asking are, "Can I trust you?" and "Do you care about me?" To be someone who people want to follow, you have to be someone they can trust—someone who cares about the people you lead. To unite others, you have to be someone people want to rally around. To connect with others, you have to be someone who creates connections.

Love Does

Leadership begins with love. Bob Goff, the author of *Love Does*, says that love is not a noun. It's a verb. It's about leading with and sharing love. It's about putting love into action. Bob wrote a bestselling book and he has lived a life worth writing about. Goff is the founder of Love Does, a nonprofit that fights the injustices committed against children. Goff has spent years working to rescue underage girls from the bondage of sexual slavery. He has worked against forced prostitution in India by arresting over 80 criminals and placing trafficked children in temporary and permanent housing. He has frequently traveled to Uganda, where he has risked his life bringing over 200 trials to court to relieve children of imprisonment. Goff and Love Does also built a school, Restore Leadership Academy, that serves over 250 children in the war-torn area of northern Uganda. When people ask me to describe Goff, I say he's a combination of Indiana Jones and Jesus. He travels around the world taking on witch doctors, criminals, and injustice while being one of the most loving, positive leaders I've ever met. When Goff is not spending time with his wife, whom he calls "Sweet Maria," he's traveling to Uganda, saving children, speaking to audiences, and answering calls on his cell phone from complete strangers because he put his cell phone number in the back of his book. Yes, he actually put his cell phone number in the book. I know because I called it to see if he would answer. He did. Why did he put his number in the book? It's the same reason why he does everything: because that's what love does. Goff said most people usually call and say, "Bob, is that really you?" And when he says yes, they say they loved his book and thanks for answering and then hang up. He said people just want to know that he's for real. From seeing Goff in action it's clear that since they know his love is real, they follow with passion and loyalty. It's the same with you as a leader. Your people want to know if you are for real. Show them you are by the way you love them.

Love Is the Greatest Leadership Principle on the Planet

Goff and many of the positive leaders I have met demonstrate that love is the greatest leadership principle on the planet. I was recently speaking to a school district and met a principal whom everyone loves and admires. She turned around her school from being an at-risk school to a model school in her district. I asked her the secret. She said, "I love my staff and students. Everything I do is to make them better." I was at a sales conference and met a gentleman who was the top salesperson in the company. I asked him his secret. He said, "I love my clients and they know it." I was visiting a professional sports team that the coach had transformed from a perennial loser into a perennial winner. I asked some of the players what the secret was. They said it was coach: "He loves the game. He loves us. We are like a family." Regardless of title or profession, to be human is to love and want to be loved. We are who we are because someone loved us and our team will be impacted by our love. Love is what separates good and great. Good teachers know their lesson plans. Great teachers know and love their students. Good coaches know X's and O's. Great coaches know and love their players. Good salespeople know how to sell. Great salespeople love their clients. Good leaders know their vision and purpose. Great leaders also know and love their people. If you want to build a great team, business, family, school, or organization, love the people you lead and work with.

Positive Leaders Build Great Relationships and Teams

Rules without Relationship Lead to Rebellion

Andy Stanley once said, "Rules without relationship lead to rebellion." Far too many leaders share rules with the people they lead but they don't have a relationship with them. So what happens? The people they lead disengage from the mission and vision of the organization. I've had many leaders tell me that when they focus less on rules and invest more in their relationships they experience a dramatic increase in performance, morale, and engagement. If you are in education, research shows that when principals have a relationship with their teachers, engagement rises; when students have a relationship with their teachers, test scores go up.[11] In sports, players will play harder for their coaches when they know the coaches love them. In business, if a client knows their representative, agent, or salespeople care about them, they will never leave and will refer everyone they know to them. Success comes down to people and relationships and building something together. When you love someone, you take the time to invest in a relationship with them to help them improve and grow. People can tell when you have an agenda, so don't have one. Just build great relationships and build something great together.

Communication Builds Trust

If you love someone, you take the time to invest in a relationship with them. To invest in a relationship with them, you must communicate with them. Relationships are the foundation upon which great teams and organizations are built, and communication serves as the initial foundation in building a great relationship. Unfortunately, most relationships and teams break down because of poor communication. In a world where we have more ways to communicate, we are communicating less meaningfully and our relationships, teamwork, and overall engagement and performance are suffering. Communication builds trust. Trust generates commitment. Commitment fosters teamwork, and teamwork delivers great results. If you don't have communication, you don't have the commitment and trust you need to build a great team and create the future together.

I was having dinner with Doc Rivers, the head coach of the Los Angeles Clippers, and I asked Doc what was the most important thing he does as a coach. He said, "I communicate to my team. Not just collectively as a team but individually. I have to know where each person is in order to lead them where I need them to be. Since I communicate often with them, I know who is struggling with a personal issue. I know who needs encouragement. I know who needs to be challenged." I then asked Doc what he would like to improve upon as a coach. He said, "I would like to improve my communication." I was blown away. Here was a coach who was considered by many as the best communicator in sports and he wanted to get even better. It demonstrates how important communication is and how much every leader needs to focus on it. Many leaders communicate collectively and communicate with everyone at once, but I'm convinced we need to learn from Doc and spend more time, energy, and effort communicating one on one. Please know that I realize it's not easy to con-sistently have one-on-one communication with everyone in

Positive Leaders Build Great Relationships and Teams

the organization. I realize you can't meet with everyone all the time, especially if you lead a large organization. The key is to meet with your leadership team and the people you lead directly, and then make sure they are communicating well with the people they lead. If everyone does this throughout the organization, relationships, teamwork, and performance will improve. What does this look like? A principal of a school would schedule two or three 10-minute meetings each day with teachers and members of their staff. A hospital adminis-trator could do the same with their doctors and nurses, or the manager of a business could have a meeting with a few of her direct reports each week. Coach Russ Rose, the six-time National Champion women's volleyball coach at Penn State, created a communication tool he calls the 1-Minute Drill, where he calls a player into his office at various times during the season for a short one-on-one meeting. He tells them what they are doing well, what they need to work on, and here is where their focus should be during the next training cycle. He then asks if they have any questions. It's a quick effective way to provide direct and honest feedback, clarify expectations, alleviate uncertainty, and improve individual and team performance.

Where There Is a Void in Communication, Negativity Fills It

I have found that where there is a void in communication, negativity will fill it. Without great communication, negativity fills the void and it breeds and grows, resulting in nega-tive contagious energy that quickly spreads. This is why communication is also essential. It not only develops great relationships and trust, but it also prevents the spread of rumors and negative energy that can sabotage a team and organization. A few years ago, the Los Angeles Clippers faced a crisis when the owner at the time, Donald Sterling, made racist remarks. The media and the world were in a frenzy, but Doc communicated with his team like he always had. Doc built such a strong foundation that they were able to weather the storm. Weaker cultures and teams without great communication would have crumbled, but Doc and his team stayed strong together. You can't wait for a crisis to hit to start communicating with your team. You must communicate before a crisis so your foundation will be strong enough to overcome it. Make sure you make communication your number-one priority. It's often the last thing you want to do but it's the most important thing you must do. Communicate more individually and collectively.

What does filling the void look like? At 8:31 AM Monday morning, all employee weekly meetings are held and challenges, weekly goals, and hot topics are discussed. Hold daily teleconferences with a sales team to communicate obstacles, wins, and learning opportunities. Establish a daily or weekly Skype session with a leader and their virtual team that's spread out around the globe. Set a daily call at noon where a manager shares an inspirational message with everyone in his company (like *One Minute Manager* author Ken Blanchard does at his company). At home, conduct a weekly family meeting, like the one my family holds on Sundays. We talk about our family mission statement, our challenges from the past week, upcoming challenges, and

Positive Leaders Build Great Relationships and Teams

anything that's on our hearts and minds. All of these ways of filling the void look like a leader communicating frequently with his team and providing honest and transparent updates about the big changes coming their way.

Leading by Walking Around

A great way to fill voids in communication is to get out of your office and interact with the people that you lead. Whether this means visiting people in the office; eating in the cafeteria as Doug Conant, the CEO of The Campbell Soup Company, did frequently; or traveling to different cities and countries, nothing beats face-to-face communication. When you interact with your team and organization, you break down the barriers of *us* versus *them* and build *we*. You develop strong relationships, a strong team, and a strong organization.

In *You Win in the Locker Room First*, Coach Mike Smith described how each day he made a couple of trips to the training room to visit with players who were getting treatment. He always wanted them to know that he was concerned and interested in how they were doing, regardless of their practice status. Some of the best conversations he ever had with players took place in the training room. He would also visit the weight room and talk to players and assistant coaches who were getting a workout. Mike said he also made it a point to eat with his players because he felt this environment allowed for more natural conversations to take place and that he learned a lot and developed great relationships with his players just by talking to them during meals. And, of course, he spent a lot of time in the locker room and would often walk in and just look around to see who was talking to who, what the energy was like, and what the overall mood of the team was. Mike called his approach "taking the temperature of the building." He didn't read the thermostat but rather would take the pulse of the team and the energy in the building. Mike said that oftentimes, leaders will only concern themselves with the temperature of the organization when things are not going well. This can be a big miscalculation. It is just as important to know what the vibes are when things are going well. In any organization the pulse can be different every day based on what's happening. The dynamics of an organization, whether in sports or business, are always changing and, as the leader, you have to be prepared to manage the ebbs and flows that occur by taking the temperature each day. Having an accurate assessment of the mood of the building and organization at all times will allow you to make the best decisions for your team or organization. Mike said he had "thermostats" around the building. Members of the training staff, equipment managers, communications staff, and player-development team members were invaluable. When walking around, he would ask these people, "What's the temperature today?" They shared priceless information about players and Mike became aware of many different situations, both positive and negative, by having these conversations. Mike said that by asking what the temperature was, "I not only learned more about the team and who was in a bad mood, but I helped our organization operate at the highest level and deal with potentially negative issues before they impacted our culture and performance." As a leader you can't just speak to other leaders who have the same vantage point as you. You have to engage people who are closest to the potential

Positive Leaders Build Great Relationships and Teams

challenges facing your organization. You have to ask questions, listen, and learn, and then decide how to use the readings to make decisions going forward.

Listening Is Communicating

People often think of communication as talking, but it's also about listening. The best communicator is not always the most eloquent speaker, but rather the person who has the ability to listen, process the information, and use it to make decisions that are in the best interest of the team and organization. The best listeners truly hear what a person is saying and trying to convey. Having worked with Mike Smith for seven years while he was the coach of the Falcons, I noticed his greatest strength as a leader was the way he listened to his team. While visiting the facility, I always saw one of Mike's players talking to him and Mike listening intently. They knew he cared about them and, as a result, they always gave their all for him.

Research shows that when people feel like they are seen and heard there is a moistening in the eyes, and yet in 90 percent of our conversations there is no moistening in the eyes. As a positive leader, it's important to be a positive communicator and make others feel important by listening to them and truly hearing what they have to say.

Enhance Your Positive Communication

Positive leaders are also positive communicators. They communicate in such a way that they make people around them better. One of my favorite phrases, for example, is "shout praise, whisper criticism." It comes from the original Olympic Dream Team and Detroit Pistons coaches Chuck Daly and Brendan Suhr. They won NBA Championships and an Olympic gold medal, thanks to a lot of talent and great communication. They gained the trust of their players and built winning teams by praising in public and constructively criticizing in private. Shouting praise means you recognize someone in front of their peers, and whispering criticism means you coach them to get better. Both build better people and teams.

Smiling is also a big part of positive communication. When you share a real smile, it not only produces more serotonin in your brain but in the brain of the recipient of your smile. Just by smiling at someone, you are giving them a dose of serotonin, an anti-depressant. Never underestimate the power of a smile. As a positive communicator, you have the power to make someone feel better just by smiling. No matter what your job is, when you smile at someone, remember you are acting as a pharmacist giving them an antidepressant.

Positive communicators also spread positive gossip. Instead of sharing negative gossip, be the kind of communicator who spreads positive news about people. My college lacrosse teammate Mike Connelly is famous for this. Whenever you talk to him he is always praising our mutual friends. "Did you hear how awesome so and so is doing? Their kids are doing great!" He never says a negative word about anyone. He always spreads the positive news and the best part is that you know when you are not around he is likely sharing something positive, not negative, about you. It's no surprise he's been a huge success in business.

111

Positive Leaders Build Great Relationships and Teams

Positive leaders and communicators also listen to and welcome ideas and suggestions on how they can improve. They don't fear criticism. They welcome it, knowing it makes them better. They send a clear signal to their team, customers, coaches, and everyone around them that they are always willing to learn, improve, and grow. Positive communicators say "I'm open. Make me better. Let's get better together." I did this to my wife one time when she wanted to give me parenting advice. Instead of being defensive, I listened. She was surprised and, after a few short hours of telling me how I can improve, I put some of her ideas into practice and made myself and my children better.

I also believe positive leaders and communicators rely on nonverbal communication. They encourage through nods, facial expressions high-fives, handshakes, pats on the back, fist bumps, and even hugs when appropriate. Positive communication isn't just verbal. It's also physical. Several studies have demonstrated the benefits of physical contact between doctors and patients, teachers and students, and professional athletes. For example, in one study the best NBA teams were also the touchiest (high-fives, pats on the back, hugs). In a world where physical touch has become taboo because of misuse and abuse, we must remember that it is a way we humans communicate naturally and is very powerful and beneficial when done *appropriately with good intention*.[12] Personally, I'm a fist bumper and a hugger. When I meet people at speaking engagements I give them a choice: bump or hug. Whichever they are more comfortable with is great with me.

Be an Encourager

Truett Cathy, the founder of Chick-Fil-A, asked rhetorically, "How do you know if a man or woman needs encouragement?" His response: "If they are breathing." We all need encouragement and positive communicators encourage and inspire others to do more and become more than they ever thought possible. Positive leaders are great encouragers and it's something the world needs more of. With so many people telling us we can't succeed, we need to hear people telling us we can. I remember my high school English teacher telling me not to apply to Cornell University because they wouldn't accept me and, even if they did, I wouldn't be able to do the work. (It's funny that I'm a writer now.) I almost didn't apply, but a few days later I saw Ivan Goldfarb, a former teacher, in the hallway and asked him about Cornell. He said, "You apply. If you get in, then you go. You can do it." His words made all the difference. I applied, was accepted, and majored in *lacrosse*. Too often we think it's our role to inject a dose of "reality" into someone's life. We think it's our job to protect people from the pain of failure and defeat. We think that dreams were meant for others. I say there are enough pessimists and realists in the world. The world doesn't need more negativity and impossible thinkers. The world needs more optimists, encouragers, and inspirers. The world needs more people to speak into the hearts of others and say, "I believe in you. Follow your passion and live your purpose. If you have the desire then you also have the power to make it happen. Keep working hard. You're improving and getting better. Keep it up. The economy is tough but you can still grow your business. The job market is not great, but I believe you'll find the right job for you. We've hit a lot of obstacles, but we'll get the project finished. Even if you fail, it will lead to something even better. You're learning and growing." We all love working for and with people who bring out the best in us. We love being around people who uplift us and make us feel great. And while we'll always remember the negative people who told us we couldn't accomplish something, we will always cherish and hold a special place in our heart for those who encouraged us. I want to encourage you to be an encourager. Leadership, as I wrote earlier, is a transfer of belief. Today, decide to be that person who instills a positive belief in someone who needs to hear your encouraging words. Uplift someone who is feeling down. Fuel your team with your positive energy. Rally others to focus on what is possible rather than what seems impossible. Share encouragement. It will help build your relationships. It matters and we all need it.

Believe in Others More than They Believe in Themselves

I'll never forget the time I tried to quit lacrosse during my freshman year in high school but my coach, Tony Caiazza, wouldn't let me. He told me that I was going to play in college one day. He even said I would play in the Ivy League. I didn't even know what the Ivy League was at the time. He had a vision for me that I couldn't even fathom. He believed in me more than I believed in myself. I ended up going to

Cornell University to play for Coach Richie Moran, who also believed in me, and the experience changed my life forever. The difference between success and failure is belief, and so often this belief is instilled in us by someone else. Coach Caiazza was that person for me and it changed my life. You can be that person for the people you lead if you believe in them and see their potential rather than their limitations. It's amazing what people will accomplish when they know you believe in them!

Help Your Team Become Unstoppable

Since I played lacrosse in college I encouraged my daughter to play as well. But in elementary school, it didn't look like she had a future in lacrosse. While the rest of the kids were running up and down the field she would stand still, pick grass, and look up at the sky. It was honestly very frustrating to watch. In middle school she started to get into the action a little more and I saw signs of life. We would often throw the ball around together and work on her stick skills. I saw improvement in practice, but when she would play in the games she was very tentative. I had to admit I wasn't a very positive leader at the time, and by pushing my expectations and frustrations on her, I almost caused her to quit playing. I was a classic transactional parent, where my identity was tied to her success. I read Joe Ehrmann's book *Inside Out Coaching*, which is about being transformational instead of transactional, and it changed me as a parent. I still played and practiced with my daughter to help her improve, but this time I did so

Positive Leaders Build Great Relationships and Teams

with encouragement instead of frustration. In ninth grade she made the high school varsity team and even started a few games, but was benched because she missed a few passes in key games. I continued to encourage her. We would practice her dodges in the backyard often and she really improved, but she was still tentative and never tried to dodge and score in the games. I started to tell her she was unstoppable all the time. I would say "You are unstoppable, Jade. They can't stop you. Take it to the goal. You are unstoppable." This was funny because at the time she was very stoppable. In the 10th grade she became a starter once again but was benched after not playing well in one or two games. I knew she had it in her to be great but she wasn't showing it. The old me would have yelled at her but the new me just encouraged her and kept telling her she was unstoppable. "Just take it to the cage and shoot, Jade. They can't stop you. You are unstoppable." I said it often and she would just smile. I kept hoping and praying she would realize her potential, unsure if it would ever happen. During her junior year I kept practicing with her and encouraging her and telling her she was unstoppable. And then finally she became unstoppable. She scored 80 goals that season, 8 in the district finals and 7 in the state semifinals, to help her team make it to the state finals. She was named an Academic All American and received offers to play lacrosse in college. It was so enjoyable to watch her play and rewarding to know that we did it the right way. I had to experience the power of positive leadership firsthand before I could write a book on it. From almost ruining my daughter, to becoming a positive leader who encouraged and believed in her, I know the difference it makes.

Connect One on One

While communication and encouragement builds trust and develops the relationship, connecting is where trust is earned, the bond is created, the relationship is strengthened, commitment is generated, and great coaching and leadership happens. Positive leaders do more than just communicate, they connect heart to heart. I spoke in the previous chapter about how leaders create a united and connected organization and team, but organization and team connection is the result of individual connection. The greatest leaders I've been around connect with those they lead. I've watched the way Cori Close, the basketball coach at UCLA; Sherri Coale, the basketball coach at Oklahoma University; and Deanna Gumpf, the Notre Dame softball coach lead and interact with their teams. I've seen how they communicate, connect, and treat their players like family. I know how much time and effort they make to connect with each player and it's why they have built successful programs over time. Without connection you'll never have commitment, but when you connect, you generate the commitment that leads to greater performance and success. I'm convinced you can't truly coach someone to grow unless you know and have a relationship with them. Connection and relationships are what drive real growth.

I witnessed a great example of a coach connecting with his player while visiting the Los Angeles Dodgers the day before they clinched a spot in the postseason in 2016. I had spoken to the coaches and team during spring training about how to build a winning team and the importance of being a connected team. Now here I was, six months later, sitting and

Positive Leaders Build Great Relationships and Teams

talking with the manager, Dave Roberts, in his office, when one of his players walked in to say hello. Dave got up from his chair and gave the player a big bear hug for about five seconds. It was the kind of hug that a dad would give his son after returning home from a long trip. They talked for a little bit about life and practice before the player said I'll see you later and left. I told Dave how great it was that he would give his player a hug like that. He said, "I do it each day and he often stops by to talk about life and challenges and whatever is on his mind." A few weeks later, while watching the Dodgers play the Nationals in the postseason I watched in amazement as this player hit home runs in Games 4 and 5 to help the Dodgers advance. It was as if I had a front-row seat to see the impact of what happens when a coach makes the time to pour love and support into one of his players. This player who had struggled the year before was now one of the heroes because his leader took the time to connect and care about him. Dave's commitment to connect wasn't isolated to just this one player. As Dave showed me around the facility, I watched as he had meaningful and frequent touch points and connections with every player and coach we encountered. It was fun and special to watch positive leadership in action.

Be Committed

Communication, encouragement, belief, listening, and connecting are essential to build great relationships and great teams, but without commitment nothing great will ever be built or accomplished. Every leader wants committed people on their team. We all want a committed team. But if you want commitment, you must be committed. If you want commitment from your team, you must show your commitment to your team. You can't just talk about your commitment. They must feel your commitment. When the people you lead see and feel your commitment, they will be more committed to you and each other. When leaders complain to me that their teams aren't committed, I always tell them to show their team what commitment looks like: "Go above and beyond. It starts with you."

"What does it look like?" they ask.

"It looks like putting the needs of others before your own."

Serve to Be Great

A team feels a leader's commitment when the leader takes the time to serve them. Jesus washed feet; Martin Luther King marched, went to jail, and fought for equality; Mother Teresa fed the poor and healed the sick. Over the years, I have met many leaders who served their teams in simple, powerful ways. Many leaders think that, as they gain power and responsibility, their teams should serve them more, but positive leaders know that their job is to serve their teams. When you serve the team, you help them grow and they help you grow. You can't serve yourself and your team at the same time. You have to decide whether you are going to serve *me* or *we*. You must decide if you are going to be a self-serving "leader" or a true leader who serves others.

It's hard to be a positive servant-leader in today's world. Leaders are under more pressure than ever to perform. If you

Positive Leaders Build Great Relationships and Teams

are a business leader, you must answer to the stock market, the board, and shareholders. If you are a coach, you must answer to your owner, general manager, and fan base. If you are a school leader you have to answer to your school board, superintendents, and parents of students. With expectations come pressure and stress that drive a leader to survive, which leads to self-preservation rather than serving the team. When leaders become focused on the fruit instead of the root, when they worry about the outcome instead of the process of developing team members, they may survive in the short run, but they will not thrive in the long run. Self-serving leaders don't leave legacies that change the world for the better. They may make money and achieve some fame in the short run, but true greatness is achieved when a leader brings out the greatness in others. Great leaders are great servants. A great leader sacrifices and serves in order to help team members become great. At the end of the day, it all comes down to this: You don't have to be great to serve, but you have to serve to be great. The big questions you must ask yourself each day are: What am I doing to serve my team and the people I lead? How can I serve them to help them be the best versions of themselves? How can I demonstrate my commitment to them? These were questions I had to ask myself and lead to lessons I needed to learn in order to be a better leader.

Doing the Laundry

A few years ago my son came to my office while I was writing a new book and asked me to play ping-pong. I said I was too busy. He came back again and again. I finally said, "I can't. I'm writing a book about engaged relationships." Here I was writing a book about engaged relationships and I was too busy to make time for the most important relationships of all!

Each year, I choose a word for the year and I knew that year my word was going to be "serve." I had been traveling a lot to speak to a number of companies, schools, and sports teams, and my wife and teenage children were struggling at home. I realized I needed to be more committed to my team and start serving at home. So I turned down a number of speaking engagements to make more time with my family. It turned out to be the hardest year of my life. My daughter was not doing great in school. My wife and son were butting heads. My wife was stressed and having trouble managing it all. It was very frustrating because I wanted my kids to be self-starters like I was as a kid. I wanted my wife to be able to handle it all. Why did they need my help? Why couldn't I just focus on making a difference in the world? Why couldn't I have a different team? Yes, I admit it. I wanted a different team. Have you ever wanted a different team? If you are a leader, coach, or parent I know the answer is yes. Despite my frustration, I made the time to help my team get better. I drove my daughter to school each day and encouraged her. When she came home, I grilled her on her homework assignments and test topics to make sure she was preparing and studying. I put the kids to bed and prayed with them. I did the laundry often. I got very involved in their everyday challenges. In short, I became committed. At the end of the year, my wife asked me what my word would be for the coming year. She asked if it was going to be "selfish," because she had never seen me do so much for my family. I told her no way. "Serve" was now a part of me and my commitment. Making the time to serve my family was how I showed I was truly committed to them. I realized that I didn't need a different team. I needed to become a better leader. Everything in my being wanted to focus on *me*, but I was at my best when I focused on *we*. I also realized a great truth for leaders: We have the team we have for a reason. The challenges we have with our team are meant to make us better leaders. In the process of committing to my family and learning to serve, I became a better leader. Ironically, that's when my books and career took off.

When you are committed, your team notices. My son hurt his back playing tennis and my wife took him to the chiropractor, who asked how I was doing. My wife told him I was speaking at the World Leaders Conference with a bunch of famous people. The chiropractor said, "Well, Jon is kind of famous." My son replied, "Not in our house. He does the laundry." When my wife told me this story I lit up. My son noticed my commitment at home and that meant everything. At the end of the day, I don't want to be a household name. I want to be a big name in my household. My daughter is also doing great at school, my wife is much happier, and I'm helping my son become the best version of himself. I believe all success starts with making the team (home team, work team, sports team) around you better.

It's Not About You

I first met Carl Liebert when he was the CEO of 24 Hour Fitness and invited me to speak to the leaders of his company. Liebert was a graduate of the Naval Academy and played on the Navy basketball team with David Robinson. After a long and successful career with Home Depot, Liebert brought his servant leadership approach to 24 Hour Fitness. Before he became CEO, the executives of 24 Hour Fitness had personal trainers visit their homes to train them in private, but Liebert made it mandatory for the executives to train at the centers so they could spend more time interacting with staff members and identify better ways to serve their team and customers. He also required executives to work for a week in one of their locations each year. Some executives chose to work in membership sales while others worked as physical trainers or in membership services. The experience helped the 24 Hour Fitness leaders to not only better serve their team but also to understand the needs of their members. It demonstrated their commitment to everyone, and it made all the difference. After successfully transforming 24 Hour Fitness, Liebert became the COO of USAA Insurance, where he continues to demonstrate his servant leadership and commitment. I have spent time at USAA and have personally witnessed the way he leads his team with authenticity, humility, and commitment. He asks for input and invites feedback. He shares his one word with everyone in the company and invites everyone to share their words with him. He looks for ways to develop the strengths of each team member and coaches them to be the best versions of

Positive Leaders Build Great Relationships and Teams

themselves. Most of all, he leads with humility, knowing it's not about him—it's about his team. He doesn't like when I write about him because he doesn't seek recognition, but I had to tell you about him because his example is so powerful. Remember, it's not about you. It's about committing yourself to others.

Commit to Coach

One of the reasons why I write a lot about coaches is because I spend a lot of time with them, and one of the reasons why I spend time with them is because I love the way great coaches commit to their teams. Everyone talks about the brilliant minds of coaches like San Antonio Spurs head coach Greg Popovich or New England Patriots head coach Bill Belichick, but if you look closer and spend time in their locker rooms, you would find that their real secret is their commitment to coaching their players to be their best. They give everything they have to help their players become all they can be. They invest in them as people and performers, helping them improve in all facets of their life. The media wouldn't describe them as positive leaders, but their players know they are. Leaders beyond sports need to learn to coach as well. I often tell leaders that you can't coach everyone in the organization but you can coach your leadership team to be better leaders and encourage them to coach their direct reports and so on throughout the organization. If every leader committed to coaching people, then performance, productivity, and profits would soar! Years ago the Army would send its best men to the elite 75th Ranger Regiment, but only about 30 percent would make it through. Army leadership decided to invest more to prepare candidates for the challenging training. The following year, 80 percent became Rangers. The difference was coaching and an investment in people, process, and preparation. When you selflessly commit to coaching, those you lead will also create a culture of coaching in your organization, and everyone benefits.

Commitment Requires Sacrifice

To build a great team and organization and to change the world, people have to know and feel that you would run into a burning building to save them. They have to know that you are willing to sacrifice yourself for their gain. Positive leaders don't just share a positive vision and take the easy road to get there. They often ignore the easy path and take the more difficult road filled with service and sacrifice. When I think of the positive leaders who changed the world, they were all committed to people. They were committed to others and a cause greater than themselves. Long before Rosa Parks decided not to give up her seat on a bus to a white man in 1955, she had been an activist. Since 1943, she had been a member of her local NAACP chapter, and she had marched on behalf of injustices in our country. She would go on to say about her decision to not give up her seat, "The only tired I was, was tired of giving in," and her simple act and commitment to others and a cause she believed in, kickstarted the civil rights movement.

Mother Teresa committed her life to serving the poorest of the poor and built her start-up missionary community of 13 members in Calcutta into a global force for good of over 4,000 nuns running orphanages, serving the poor, and healing the sick. A winner of the Nobel Peace Prize, she inspired countless people to serve and she showed the world what commitment looks like.

On the surface it looks like Oprah built herself a fortune by focusing on her needs and taking the easy path, but this couldn't be further from the truth. Yes, she built a media empire, but it was her perseverance, grit, and commitment to helping people grow that made her empire possible. Maya Angelou said, "A leader sees greatness in other people. He nor she can't be much of a leader if all she sees is herself." Positive leaders see others and commit to bringing out the greatness in others.

When You Help Others Improve, You Improve

The great thing about commitment is that when you commit your life to helping others grow, you grow. Swen Nater was an All American at Cypress Community College when John Wooden recruited him to play at UCLA. As the story goes, Wooden told him that he wasn't going to play in a lot of games because they already had the best center in the world in Bill Walton, but Nater would have the opportunity to play against Walton every day in practice. Wooden wanted the six-foot-eleven Nater to challenge and push Walton to improve. Nater accepted his role during his time at UCLA and every day in practice he focused on one task: making Walton better. While he was helping Walton improve, something interesting happened. Nater also improved. He was the only player in ABA and NBA history to be drafted in the first round never having started a collegiate game. Nater was named the ABA Rookie of the Year and went on to have a 12-year career in the ABA and NBA. He is a great example of how, when you help your team get better, you get better. When you focus on helping others improve, you improve. When you lose your ego in the service of others, you find the greatness within you. Great leaders serve the people they lead. Nater's commitment to his team helped him become a successful professional basketball player, and he's now an executive with Costco, where he's making everyone around him better. There are countless ways to help others improve. I can't tell you what you should do, but I can tell you that when you commit to being a positive leader dedicated to others, you will be well on your way to transforming your team and the world.

Elite of the Elite

I met a leader of Special Forces for the United States, and he told me how Navy Seals have to try out to be members of the elite group Seal Team Six. While Navy Seals are considered to be elite members of Special Forces, they have to try out to be members of the elite Seal Team Six unit. He said that, while prospects are trying out, the current team is looking for certain characteristics. If during the tryout a prospect doesn't fit their criteria, Seal Team Six says, "Thank you very much, but you're not the right fit."

"What's the right fit?" I asked. He said what we are looking for is not just someone who performs at the highest level but, while performing at the highest level also looks out for his team members, making them better in the process. It occurred to me that if you want to be elite you can be a high performer, but if you want be the elite of the elite you have to be a transformational positive leader and a high performer who makes others better in the process.

Positive Leaders Care

It all comes down to caring. If you don't love, you don't care, and if you don't care, you won't make the time to unite, communicate, encourage, connect, commit, serve, or sacrifice. Positive leaders care about the people they lead. They care about their team and organization. They care about changing the world because they know the world needs changing. Because they care, they do more, give more, encourage more, help more, guide more, mentor more, develop more, build more, and, ultimately, accomplish more. If I had a dollar for every time I heard the saying, "People don't care how much you know until they know how much you care," I would be rich. But the reason why people say it so much is because it's true. When you care about someone, they know it and feel it. And when they know you care about them, they will care about you and follow you with loyalty and passion. Pat Summitt, the legendary women's basketball coach at Tennessee, said, "I won 1,098 games and eight national championships, and coached in four different decades. But what I see are not the numbers. I see their faces." And her players still talk about how she cared about the faces she saw. She became a surrogate mother to hundreds of her players over the years—players who became more like her daughters. What they remember most about her was the way she cared about them and made time for them and always had her office door open so they could walk in and sit down and talk with her. One of her players, Candace Parker, said Summitt was excited about winning championships but she was even more excited about making a difference in the lives of her players.

Develop Your Caring Trademark

Great leaders have what I call a *caring trademark*, a unique way that shows they care that causes them to stand out in their work and in the world. If you've followed Derek Jeter's career and watched his improbable game-winning hit in his final at bat in Yankee Stadium, you know that Derek treated every at bat like it was his last, and that's what made his last at bat so special. No one worked harder, played with more passion, or cared more about his team and honoring the game of baseball than "The Captain," Derek Jeter. Jeter's hustle, passion, love of his team, commitment, and work ethic have become his *caring trademark* over the last 20 years. While Jeter always sprinted to first base and treated every at bat as a sacred experience, Doug Conant's *caring trademark* was writing over 10,000 thank-you notes to employees while he was the CEO of Campbell Soup.

Drew Watkins, the superintendent of Prosper Independent School District (ISD) in Texas, shows he cares more than any educator I've ever met. I found out from his staff that he writes a personal note of congratulations to every graduating senior. They mentioned it casually in conversation, as if it was no big deal, but I quickly stopped in my tracks. "How many graduates do you have this year?" I asked. "403," they said. "He started doing it when we had just 80 graduates in the district and keeps doing it year after year no matter how much we grow. "I asked how he learns about each student. "Does he get a report from the teachers in order to write the notes?" "No," they said. "He actually knows them. He personally knows every student in the district. He's in the schools all the time, not his office." It was clear that he loves the students and they love him back, as you can see from the big hug he received from a big graduate.

When Watkins and I had some time to chat, I asked what he's going to do when he has 1,000 graduates. He told me he was going to keep doing it. "The day I stop is the day I need to stop doing this job," he said. "The crime is not that the passion has run out. It's that you stuck around after it has." Watkins is, in no way, just sticking around. I found out that in addition to writing notes to graduates he also sends each student in Prosper ISD a note on their birthday. He can often be seen opening car doors and greeting students in the car line each morning before school. Sometimes he leaves messages of encouragement on whiteboards in the classrooms while the teachers and students are at lunch. And every Monday morning he sends all the educators and staff in the district an email with words of wisdom, encouragement, and praise. I posted a comment on Facebook about meeting Watkins, and the comments flooded in.

A former student wrote:

I've known him since I was a kid in pre-k. He sat down with me at lunch one day my junior year in high school and asked, "Still don't like the crust?" meaning my sandwich which I had torn the crust off from. For him to remember that I didn't like the crust all this time still amazes me. I'm grateful to have had him for a superintendent, couldn't have asked for a better one.

A few moms wrote:

"I'll never forget when my children were in kindergarten. They came home talking about a 'man' that sat with them at lunch. Puzzled, I was like 'What man??!' They quickly responded, 'Mr. Watkins.' I was impressed six years ago and

Positive Leaders Build Great Relationships and Teams

have continued to be, as I see him opening car doors, greeting the kids in car line . . . sometimes in the pouring rain."

"He opened the car door for my son Jacob on his first day of kindergarten and on his last day of his senior year and he remembered!! Made me cry like a baby."

A few teachers from Prosper ISD wrote:

"I love Dr. Watkins. Twelve years working for Prosper ISD, and he has the same passion as the first day. Proud to be part of his staff."

"Dr. Watkins is a leader by example. He shows the students, staff, and the community of Prosper that he cares!!"

The overwhelming flood of responses showed how much people appreciate a leader who cares and how we long for leaders to care. I left Prosper ISD inspired by Drew Watkins to do more to show that I care. I hope after reading this you feel the same way. Drew Watkins is a great model for all of us. We can all care more, give more, and do more to make a difference. We may not rise to the level of caring of Drew Watkins, but we can strive to be more like him. We can all work to invest in relationships and find ways to show people that we care about them. When you show you care in your own unique way, you will stand out in a world where many have seemed to forget to care. And when you care, you inspire others to care. After all, think about all the great organizations lead by positive leaders who are showing the world they care. A caring leader unites, connects, encourages, and transforms teams and organizations and changes the world.

The Sandwich

The first leader I ever met, the one who was my greatest coach and encourager, the one who loved and served me and cared about me like no other was my mom. She wasn't always positive to herself but she taught me one of the greatest lessons in positive leadership. More than 10 years ago I was taking a walk with my mom near her home in South Florida when I noticed she was getting tired. My mom and I always walked together. She was a fit, walking machine and never got tired, so I knew something was wrong. "Let's go back to the condo so you can rest," I said.

"No, I want to walk to the store so I can get some food to make you a sandwich for your drive home."

I was headed back to my home in Ponte Vedra Beach and my mom thought I might starve to death without eating during the five-hour drive. Her caring trademark was cooking for me. We continued walking, made it to the supermarket, and, as we walked back, I could tell she was getting more and more tired. When we arrived back at her condo she was exhausted, and yet the first thing she did was walk into the kitchen to make me a sandwich. On my drive home, I ate her sandwich but didn't think much about it at the time. Now, over 10 years later, I think about that sandwich a lot because it was the last time I saw my mom fully conscious. My mom was battling cancer, which was why she was so tired. She didn't tell me how bad it really was, nor did she mention how bleak the odds were for her survival. She was fighting for her life and, yet, on that day, her biggest priority was to make me a sandwich. Looking back I realize she wasn't just making

133

me a sandwich. She was showing me what selfless love and positive leadership are all about. At her funeral, many of her real estate clients and colleagues came up to me and shared countless stories of all the selfless acts of love my mom did for them as well. It turns out she served her team at work and her clients the same way she served her family. We often think that great leadership is about big visions, big goals, big actions, and big success. But I learned from my mom that real positive leadership is about serving others by doing the little things with a big dose of selfless love. Many want to be big-time leaders but it's important to remember that being a big-time leader starts with doing the little things to serve those you lead. It's always about the little things. Unity, relation-ships, and teamwork are developed slowly, one day; one interaction; one moment; one loving, serving, and caring act at a time.

Chapter 9

Positive Leaders Pursue Excellence

*People think you have to choose between positivity
and winning. You don't have to choose.
Positivity leads to winning.*

P ositive leaders care about others and are optimistic about the future, so they are always looking for ways to make it better. They are always looking for ways to transform what is into what could be. They are never satisfied with the status quo and as a result are always striving to improve themselves, their teams, their organizations, and the world. They pursue excellence, build greatness, and often try to accomplish the impossible. These efforts are not for the faint of heart. They require passion, humility, grit, confidence, drive, and an uncommon desire to be ones best and bring out the best in others. Positive leaders make their life and work a quest for excellence. When they wake up, they ask themselves, "How can I get better to make the world better?" A positive leader on a quest for excellence is significant because one positive leader in pursuit of excellence raises the standards and performance of everyone around them.

Humble and Hungry

Positive leaders are humble and hungry. They don't think they know it all. They are life-long learners who are always seeking ways to learn, improve, and grow. They are always open to new ideas and strategies to take their life and work to the next level. They live with humility, knowing that the minute they think they've arrived at the door of greatness is the moment it will get slammed in their face. They are also hungry with a passion and burning desire to continuously improve and grow. They are willing to put in the sweat and tears, commitment and years in order to help their teams and organizations accomplish great things. Matt Ryan, the quarterback of the Atlanta Falcons, is a great example of humble and hungry. Every time I spoke to the team during training camp, he was always sitting in the front row to the left and would always come up to me afterwards and ask me a question about something I shared. He wasn't motivated by a paycheck. He had already signed a $100 million contract. He was always looking for even the smallest way to improve and get better as a quarterback and leader, and it's why he continues to improve every year.

Positive leaders never stop learning and growing and improving. I remember speaking at a leadership conference in Dallas and looking over to the left in the front row and seeing Zig Ziglar, the legendary motivational speaker sitting there. I ran over to him and said, "Zig, one of the big goals in my life was to meet you."

He said, "You need to have bigger goals."

He was still funny after all them years. While speaking, I looked over and saw Ziglar taking notes. At 82 years old, he was taking notes. Not because I was up there. Anybody could have been up there and he would have been taking notes. He was humble and hungry. He only lived a few more years after that but I'll always remember how he spent the last few years of his life—still improving. I love what Pablo Casals, the famous cellist, said when asked why he continued to practice the cello at the age of 90. He said, "Because I think I'm making progress."

There Is No Finish Line

While having lunch with George Raveling, the legendary Hall of Fame college basketball coach, I learned that after three decades of coaching he worked in broadcasting for a few years before joining Nike at the age of 62 years old as their director of global basketball sports marketing. While most people are getting ready to retire, George said working at Nike was like going to Harvard Business School. He learned more in the last 18 years of his life than the previous 52 years. At 80 years old George reads 50 books a year and asks himself often, what do I need to know that I don't know? What do I need to unlearn to learn? Each day his goal is to be a positive difference in as many people's lives as possible. I asked George if he would ever retire. He said, "I've thought about it but then what would I do?" He's already mentored and impacted countless coaches, players, and people but he's still not done making a difference. Reiterating one of Nike's tag lines he said, "There is no finish line." At 80 he's still learning, growing, and improving. So can you at any age. Keep learning. Keep improving. Keep helping others. Keep making a positive impact. There is no finish line.

Demanding without Being Demeaning

Many think that positive leaders are nice, undisciplined, happy-go-lucky people who smile all the time and believe that results are not important. But this couldn't be further from the truth.

Positive leaders are demanding without being demeaning. They both challenge and encourage their teams and organizations to continue to improve and get better. Being a positive leader doesn't mean you don't have high expectations. The greatest positive leaders I have met, such as Alan Mulally, have very high expectations. You don't transform a company losing $14 billon into a profitable business in a few years without high expectations. However, he provided the encouragement, process, system, and coaching to meet these expectations. Pete Carroll, coach of the Seattle Seahawks, is known for creating a culture where his team has a lot of fun but he's also one of the most competitive people you'll ever meet. His belief that competition makes you better is a huge part of the Seattle Seahawks DNA, and they are passionate about always improving and winning.

Love and Accountability

I've worked with and studied leaders for years and I believe that the positive leaders who are able to create amazing teams and results provide both a lot of love and a lot of accountability. *Love* and *accountability*. That is how great teams, organizations, relationships, and results are created. If I had to pick the most important section of the book it would be *right here*: Alan Mulally, for example, told me that you have to love your people, but you have to make sure you hold your team accountable to the plan, the process, the principles, and the values of the culture. Alan told me that while his leadership approach and management system includes bringing everyone in the company together, respect, helping and appreciating each other, having fun, and enjoying the journey, it's also about a relentless implementation of the plan. It's about having clear performance goals and making sure everyone knows the goals and knows the data, status, and progress towards those goals. It's making sure everyone knows the plan and what needs special attention. If you are having a problem, that's okay, but don't keep it a secret. Let's figure it out together and find a solution. If you are failing in some way, you won't be ostracized, but rather you will find the support you need to succeed. Yet, Alan said there is zero tolerance for violating the process. If you are not willing to work with others on the plan, then Ford is probably not the right fit for you. Alan said his number-one job was to be a keeper of the culture and hold his team accountable to the principles, values, process, and behaviors. He said if someone violates the process and you don't address it, then everyone knows you aren't committed to it. If you don't hold people accountable to it, your team won't live and breathe it. But when you love people and hold them accountable, it's amazing how fast things can move in the right direction. When Alan took over Ford, his leadership team didn't know if he was for real and many people didn't buy into his approach at first. But Alan was steadfast in his principles and process. He held his team accountable to the process and his expectations and, as a result, he quickly earned their trust and respect, and teamwork improved swiftly.

Dabo Swinney is one of the best I've ever seen at providing both love and accountability, and it's one of the key reasons for their recent success and prominence. When you spend time

Positive Leaders Pursue Excellence

with him and his program, you can feel the love he has for his players. They know it. But they also know that he's there to make them better and hold them accountable to the standards they have set at Clemson. Clemson is like a big family with a lot of love and also a lot of structure and discipline. When one of his star players violated team rules, Dabo wouldn't let him play the first game of the season against Auburn, a very good team. Although it wasn't a big violation, and most teams would have let the player play, Dabo told me, "We have to hold everyone accountable to the standards we have set, and if I let him play what does that say to our players, our staff, our university, and our fans? We have our values and we must live them." People tried to convince him otherwise but he stuck to his guns and they won the game without their star player. That was five years before Clemson would win a National Championship. To understand how important the culture, values, and process are to Dabo, he has a book about 18 inches thick with ideas, principles, beliefs, cultural values, and other notes that he reviews with his coaching staff during a four-day retreat before the season. Every year, for four full days, Dabo goes through the book, page by page, with his staff. He said, "You can't assume they know it or remember it. You can't forget all the little things that made and make you successful. You have to go back to the basics and that's what we do for four full days. This book represents the foundation of what we are all about and we commit to it. Then we love our players and hold them accountable to it." Love without accountability means you'll have great relationships and be a loving family, but you won't be a great team. On a great team, each player makes the others better. Everyone strives for excellence together and accomplishes great things together. If you have accountability without love, you won't have real commitment, buy-in, loyalty, passion, or great teamwork. You'll be more like a dysfunctional family that fights all the time and simply tries to survive each day but doesn't thrive. Eventually the rules will lead to rebellion and the pressure and stress without support will lead to burnout.

Love Tough

The difference between a positive leader and other leaders is that many leaders focus on accountability first and love comes later or not at all. Many talk about tough love and I believe in it, but I have found that love must come first. If your team knows you love them, they will allow you to challenge and push them. Instead of tough love, it needs to be *love tough*. My friend Buzz Williams, who is the head basketball coach at Virginia Tech, loves his players and invests in them so much that he earns the right to push them beyond their comfort zone to be their best. He helps them become better than they ever thought possible because he's all about love tough. John Calipari is the same way. And so is Stephanie White, Christine Halfpenny, Brad Stevens, Mike Matheny, and Clint Hurdle—so are all the positive leaders who make the greatest impact. When you think about it, it's not a *nice* way to lead, but rather it's *the* way to lead, because when you love someone you want to help them improve. It means you challenge them to reach their full potential. You don't let them settle for anything but their best. Your team may not like you for it now, but they will appreciate you for it later. I tell this to my teenagers all the time because they are the beneficiaries of my *love tough* leadership. And I know from experience that your team won't hate you if your love comes first. They may not like it but they will know you love them and want the best for them.

Craftsmen and Craftswomen

Positive leaders help their team become craftsmen and craftswomen instead of carpenters. There's a difference between a carpenter and a craftsman. A carpenter just builds something but a craftsman puts in more time, energy, effort, and care to build a work of art. Instead of just showing up and going through the motions, a craftsman works to build masterpieces. In a world where too many settle for mediocrity, craftsmen and craftswomen seek to create excellence and build greatness. They care more and, because they care more, they invest more—more energy, effort, sweat, tears, and years mastering their craft. While speaking to an MLB baseball team in their locker room I asked them how many believed they could work harder than they already were. Everyone raised their hands. Then I said, "So what's the next question?"

They answered "Why aren't you?"

We discussed it and decided that to work harder, you have to care more. If you care more, you will put your heart, soul, spirit, and passion into it to accomplish more. If you care more about your project, work, and craft than about all the distractions vying for your attention, you won't allow those distractions to get in the way. You will invest your energy into building something meaningful that lasts. Positive leaders and their teams care more and, as a result, they create more masterpieces.

In Walter Isaacson's biography of Steve Jobs, he shared a story about Jobs as a young boy helping his father build a fence. His father told him he must care about crafting the back of the fence as much as the front. When Steve asked why the back mattered when no one would see how it was crafted, his father said, "But, you will know." Steve's father taught him to care more and, years later, he went on to create Apple products with such care that they generated feelings of awe, loyalty, and passion among the brand's millions of new customers. It wasn't an accident. Jonathan Ive, the man who has designed many iconic Apple products, said, "We believe our customers can sense the care we put into our products." Apple cared about the work they did and the products they created and, in turn, their customers cared about them. I know Steve Jobs wasn't considered very positive by most who worked with him, and some would argue that he wouldn't be considered a positive leader. Please keep in mind that no one is a perfect positive leader and not everyone has every trait discussed in this book. From all accounts, Jobs fell short in his ability to develop relationships, but his vision, mission, optimism, pursuit of excellence, and desire to change the world were unmatched, and that's why I am sharing what he did. He was a craftsman who cared more, and I believe it was his passion that attracted people to him and inspired them to be craftspeople who created masterpieces that changed the world.

The One Percent Rule

It's a simple rule I share with leaders and teams to help them create excellence. The rule says to give one percent more time, energy, effort, focus, and care today than you gave yesterday. Each day give more than you did the day before. Obviously you can't calculate one percent, but you can push yourself more today than you did yesterday. You can improve and get better today. You can strive for excellence and work to become your best. You can tune out distractions and focus even more on what matters most. I've had one team with 35 people implementing the one percent rule. They said if each person gives one percent more each day that's 35 percent daily and, over time, this extra percent will produce big results. It did. They had incredible growth by pursuing both individual and team excellence.

Clarity and Action

Excellence is what positive leaders strive for, but you can't achieve excellence without clarity and action. Positive leaders provide the clarity that leads to focused action. This was never more clear to me than when Alan Mulally shared several images with me before our conversation. One image included his Working Together management system, principles, and practices that are a list of 11 expected ideals, such as "people first," "everyone is included," and "clear performance goals." The second image featured Mulally's Creating Value Roadmap process, which shared the process and strategy he and his team and organization would utilize to work together to relentlessly implement the plan. Every key part of the process and plan were all contained in one image that provided the clarity of vision, process, focus, and plan. The third image Mulally shared was also Ford's Creating Value Roadmap process. This time he had designed it for Ford. On a two-sided plastic card that was shared with everyone in the company, Mulally included the vision, strategy, and plan: One Ford. One team. One plan. One goal. Mulally said that everyone needs to know the plan, embrace the plan, and trust the process. Then you love 'em up and let them take action. When I spoke with Mulally, he said everything he did was based on these three images, which everyone knew, understood, and embraced. I immediately saw the genius in his approach and management system. Everything everyone needed to know was right there in front of them in a card they could hold in their hand. They didn't have to search the company website for it or read a 200-page book. Everyone had the plan, knew the plan, and understood the process. Mulally provided such clarity that it enabled and empowered everyone in the company to take action. There was no ambiguity creating hesitancy, or clutter slowing people down. Instead, there was organizational unity, operational discipline, and focused action day after day, week after week, that over time produced incredible results.

As a leader, don't fall into the trap that the idea or plan has to be complicated to work. Simple is powerful. Clarity leads to focus and action. Action leads to results. You can be the most positive leader, but optimism without action equals today's fantasy. Optimism plus clarity and action equals tomorrow's reality. Through love and accountability, clarity and action, and a relentless drive to improve and succeed, positive leaders transform their quest for excellence into a better future for all.

Chapter 10

Positive Leaders Lead with Purpose

We don't get burned out because of what we do.
We get burned out because we forget why we do it.

T here will be days that you wake up and don't feel very positive. There will be times your culture doesn't seem strong. There will be moments you don't feel very positive about the vision of where you are going. There will be meetings where the energy vampires seem like they have the upper hand. There will be conversations where you don't feel like communicating and connecting. There will be nights where you wonder why you chose a leadership position at all. It's times like these where you need a purpose to give you something to be positive about. Purpose fuels positivity and is the reason why you overcome all the challenges and keep moving forward. Purpose is why you wake up and want to transform your team and organization and change the world. Without a greater purpose, there's no great desire. Every great organization must have a greater purpose for why they exist and every positive leader must be driven by purpose to lead others and make a greater impact. Donna Orender, for example, told me that her optimism to transform and improve the PGA Tour and WNBA came from finding the greater purpose that drives her motivation. Motivation doesn't last, but purpose-driven motivation does. Trying to lead without purpose is like driving from New York to California on a half a tank of gas.

You'll be running on empty before you know it. But knowing, remembering, and living your purpose is like having a series of gas stations along the journey. You can fuel up and keep moving forward.

People think that hard work is what makes us tired. Hard work doesn't make us tired. A lack of purpose is what makes us tired. We don't get burned out because of what do. We get burned out because we forget why we do it. Research shows that more people die Monday morning at 9 AM than any other time. Think about it. People would rather die than go to work. We live in a world where many are seeking happiness but they are having trouble finding it. That's because happiness isn't an outside job. It's an inside job. It doesn't come from the work you do but rather from the meaning and purpose you bring to your work. That's why I want to encourage you not to seek happiness. Live your passion and purpose, and happiness will find you. Don't chase success. Instead, decide to make a difference with a greater purpose, and success will find you.

Alan Mulally didn't transform Ford just because he created organizational unity and operational discipline, and because everyone knew the plan, embraced the plan, and worked toward the plan. He also transformed Ford because he inspired everyone with a greater purpose. It was a purpose that inspired Henry Ford from the very beginning, and it was to *open the highways to all of mankind*. Alan simply had to remind everyone in the company why they existed and then he had to live with purpose, which he did in a big way, and inspire purpose in others. Alan was also driven with purpose to make a significant contribution to the world and, by saving Ford, an American icon, and saving tens of thousands of jobs and contributing to the U.S. and global economies, he certainly did. As a leader you need to know, remember, and live your why and inspire the people on your team in your organization to do the same. When you are driven with purpose you will inspire others to drive with purpose.

Find and Live Your Purpose

It starts with you and your purpose as a leader. Why do you lead? Why do you do the work you do? If you don't have a purpose you can't share it. I wrote a book, *The Seed*, about finding your purpose. Josh, the main character, doesn't have a purpose. He meets a farmer who gives him a seed and tells him to find out where to plant the seed. When he finds the right place, he will find his purpose. Josh goes on a journey to plant his seed, ultimately learning that he needs to plant the seed right where he is. He discovers that when you plant yourself where you are and decide to make a difference and live with purpose, your greater purpose starts to reveal itself to you.

Tamika Catchings didn't become one of the all-time great leaders and a WNBA basketball player simply because she worked hard. She became one of the greatest because of her great desire to inspire people and change the world through her sport. Rhonda Revelle didn't win more than 700 games as the softball coach at Nebraska just because she pursued excellence. She did it because she was driven with purpose to make a difference in the lives of her players off and on the field. The research shows that people are most energized when they are using their strengths for a bigger purpose beyond themselves.[13]

I can't tell you what your purpose should be, but I can tell you that every one of us can find a bigger purpose in the job we have. I met a mortgage broker at a conference who told me that her job is to save marriages. "How do you do that?" I asked, wondering how this was possible as a mortgage broker. She said during the great recession we found that if people lost their homes their marriage was more likely to fall apart. "So I made it my mission to help people find ways to keep their home so they can keep their marriage intact." It's no surprise she was number one in her company. I heard about a janitor who worked at NASA and, even though he was sweeping floors, he felt his bigger purpose was contributing to put a man on the moon. I met a bus driver who knows his purpose was to help kids stay off drugs. I met an administrative assistant who has become the chief energy officer of her company. I met an Atlanta Airport Popeye's Chicken employee named Edith who makes thousands of air travelers smile each day. I know my purpose is to inspire and empower as many people as possible, one person at a time. We are all just ordinary people with the power to live an extraordinary purpose. In any job, your purpose waits for you to find it and live it.

A friend of mine who is a human resources executive at a children's hospital told me that once a week she sits in the lobby of the hospital to see the patients and their families and remind herself why the work she does matters. If she didn't, she said, she would get lost in all of the paperwork, HR issues, and distractions that seem far removed from the core mission of helping to heal children. But by sitting in the lobby and connecting to her purpose, she is able to do those mundane tasks knowing she is contributing to the purpose of the hospital.

Your job may not be your ultimate purpose, but through your leadership you can use it to be a vehicle to share your greater purpose. Most of all, remember that if you are a leader, you have a purpose and it's to inspire others to live theirs.

Share the Purpose

When I speak to leaders I encourage them to share a vision and purpose in one statement. I believe they are stronger together. The vision is where you are going. The purpose is why you are going there. Together, they provide you with the fuel you need on your journey. As a leader, one of the most important things you can do is share and remind the people on your team and in your organization of the greater purpose of why you exist. Why are you here? What difference can you make? What legacy will you leave? If vision is the North Star, purpose is the fuel that powers you to follow it. Everyone needs a North Star and everyone needs a bigger and greater purpose. Alan Mulally told me he shared the vision and purpose before every meeting. Steve Jobs may not have been big on positivity, but he was driven with purpose and he shared that purpose with everyone at Apple. The Pittsburgh Pirates told me their purpose is to help their players become better men, and better men become better baseball players. Everyone in the organization knows the purpose and seeks to share it.

Inspire Others to Live Their Purpose

Sharing the purpose is important but it's futile unless it inspires purpose in others. As a leader, you want to share the organizational purpose with the purpose of inspiring others to join the mission and be on a mission. You want to let everyone know why your organization exists and why their work matters. Many think they have to work at a homeless shelter or go to Africa to make a difference. They think they have to find meaning and purpose outside their work. And while it's wonderful if they want to volunteer for a charity or feel called to go on a mission trip, as a leader you want to remind your team that you don't have to go on a mission trip to be on a mission. You can bring your mission, passion, and purpose to the work that you do each day. Tell your people that you may not build libraries around the world, but you can find the bigger purpose in reading to your children. You may not feed the homeless every day, but you can nourish your employees and customers with a smile, kind word, and care. And while you may not start your own nonprofit organization, you can begin a charity initiative at work. After all, *charity* means "love in action." You can make a difference every day and touch the lives of everyone you meet. While these people may not be starving because of a lack of food, you can provide them with a different kind of nourishment that will feed their souls and feed your own in the process.

Purpose-Driven Goals

One of the great ways I have discovered to help people to live with purpose is to help them create purpose driven goals. For example, for years I chose Organic Valley milk over other brands in the supermarket. I had no idea why it appealed to me until I spoke at their remote headquarters surrounded by acres of farmland in the middle of Wisconsin. I discovered a company that didn't believe in sales and revenue goals. Of course they forecasted sales for budgetary, planning, and growth purposes, and measured numbers and outcomes, but they did so with the belief that numbers were just a byproduct of how well they were living and sharing their purpose. Instead of focusing on goals with numbers, Organic Valley passionately focused on their purpose-driven goals: providing opportunities for farmers to make a living; sustainability of the land; and providing families with healthy dairy products that were free of hormones and antibiotics. The result: Organic Valley's numbers kept growing and growing. They had a mission people could taste.

While speaking to an NFL team a few years ago, I had each player write their goals on a piece of paper. After a few minutes, I had them rip up the paper they had just written on. (I was inspired by my friend Joshua Medcalf's book *Burn Your Goals*, but didn't want to be the guy known for causing a fire in an NFL meeting room, so I had them rip up the paper instead.) You could hear the complaints and feel their anger and frustration while they ripped up the paper they had just spent time and energy writing on. I then asked, "How many of you wrote down *win a Super Bowl, win x number of games, achieve x number of yards, have x number of interceptions, etc.?*"All the hands went up. I told them that every person in every NFL meeting room has the same goals. It's not the goals that will make you successful. Otherwise everyone and every team would be successful after writing down their goals. Instead, it's your commitment to the process, your growth and your purpose that drives you to reach these goals that will determine what you accomplish. I then had them write down their

Positive Leaders Lead with Purpose

commitments and purpose for playing and had them share with the rest of the team. It was powerful.

The truth is that numbers and goals don't drive people. People with a purpose drive the numbers and achieve goals. Research clearly shows that true motivation is driven by meaning and purpose rather than extrinsic rewards, numbers, and goals. A study of West Point alums showed that those who had intrinsic goals, "I want to serve my country and make a difference" outperformed those with extrinsic goals "I want to rise in the ranks and become an officer because it's prestigious." Goals may motivate you in the short term but they will not sustain you over time.[14] Without a good reason to keep moving forward during challenges, you either quit or go through the motions.

Now this doesn't mean you shouldn't measure numbers or have goals. You need to measure the numbers. In many cases you need to have revenue targets. Numbers are to your purpose what a scale and measuring tape are to a diet. It's in indicator of how you are doing. In the case of Ford, Alan Mually had clear performance goals that were a key part of the plan and process. Every organization wants to surpass last year's number. Every nonprofit wants to help more people. Every school wants to empower more children. Every hospital wants to reduce patient deaths and save more lives. It's great to have a goal you want to achieve, but once you identify a goal or outcome, you will be more powerful and energized if you are tapping into a bigger purpose in order to reach your numbers and goals. Your greater purpose will lead to greater performance! Yes, count the fruit, but know it's just a byproduct of how well you are nurturing the root. Purpose-driven goals sell more milk, win more games, enhance performance, and lead to outcomes that far surpass your numbered goals alone.

One Word

A powerful and practical way to live with purpose throughout the year is to pick a word for the year that will inspire you to live with more meaning and mission, passion and purpose. My friends Dan Britton and Jimmy Page have been doing this for over 20 years, and the words they choose each year have shaped and inspired their lives in many ways. About six years ago, they told me how each year they, along with their family members, pick a word and, on New Year's Eve, each member of their family makes a painting of their word. They put the paintings in the kitchen as a reminder to live their word. I thought it was really powerful and started doing it as well with my family, and then shared the idea with the various leaders and teams I worked with. It was catalytic and life changing. Leaders shared words with me like, "love" and "dream" and "invest" and "go" and "execute" and "fearless" and "life" and "relationships." Dabo Swinney even said in the interview immediately after winning the National Championship, "My word all year was *love* and I told my team that their love for each other was going to make the difference." It's an idea that has taken off and now hundreds of thousands of leaders and their teams pick a word each year to inspire them at work and home. Hendrick Auto even created a one-word car in their headquarters with all the words of all the employees on the car. When employees walk into the building they see their words and are reminded to live them. I've also had schools

Positive Leaders Lead with Purpose

make one-word t-shirts and create one-world walls, and businesses and hospitals post words in meeting rooms and offices. When speaking about this idea, I ask people to pick a word but also to identify why they chose it. It's the why behind the word that gives it meaning and makes it a powerful, purpose producer. It's also a powerful exercise for leaders to do with their teams. Imagine if you and everyone you work with had a word for the year and truly lived it. How much more powerful would you be? How much of a greater impact would you make?

Life Word

In addition to choosing a word for the year I also encourage leaders to select a Life Word. When the One Word concept took off, Dan, Jimmy, and I, kept talking about ways to leave a greater legacy. While engaged in a meaningful conversation one day, we asked each other, "What word would you put on your tombstone?" We found it was a totally different thought process than coming up with a yearly word. Dan chose *passion*. Jimmy chose *inspire*. And I said *positive* because I know it's my life's work and legacy. Then we wondered what words would capture the essence and legacy of some of history's heroes. Perhaps Abraham Lincoln's Life Word would have been *unity*. Martin Luther King, Jr.'s, *equality*. Mother Teresa's *compassion*, Susan B. Anthony's *vote*. We realized that if we could help people identify their Life Word, it would inspire them to live their highest purpose and leave their greatest legacy. We have taken a bunch of leaders through the process of finding a word for the year and a Life Word, and it has been exponentially purposeful and powerful. Think of each *yearly word* as a chapter in a book, and your Life Word as the book's title. Together, they help you define and write your life's story and leave and share your greatest legacy.

Leave a Legacy

Researchers conducted a study and they asked a group of 90-year-olds if they could live their lives over again, what they would do differently. The three things that almost all of them said were:

1. They would reflect more. They would enjoy more moments, more sunrises, more sunsets, more moments of joy.

2. They would have taken more risks and chances. Life is too short not to go for it.

3. They would have left a legacy, something that would have lived on after they die.[15]

The most important legacies you will leave as a leader are people and a world that have been impacted by your leadership, life, and presence. To live a life of purpose, think about how you want to be remembered. Think about what legacy you want to leave, because knowing how you want to be remembered helps you decide how to live and lead today.

Tim Tebow is a great example of someone who is living his life to leave a legacy. He could just be enjoying his celebrity but instead he's using his fame and life to make a difference in the world through The Tim Tebow Foundation. Tebow told me that when he was cut from the Broncos, Eagles, and Jets, he didn't let it shake him because his identity was rooted in something much greater than being a football player. He knew his life's work wasn't just to be a great athlete but also to be a game changer in life, and a life changer for others. Most people know him as a Heisman Trophy winner pursuing his dream of being an NFL quarterback, but what they don't know is that he's building greatness by providing orphans in four countries with medicine, food, clothing, education, and housing. Through his foundation, he builds Timmy's Playrooms in children's hospitals, and provides medical care to countless children who can't afford it through his Tebow Cure Hospital in the Philippines. His foundation also creates an unforgettable prom night experience, A Night to Shine, for teenagers with special needs. The teenagers, who have to be 14 and older, walk into the event on a red carpet while the crowd cheers as they enter the building. Inside they are treated like kings and queens, with hair and makeup stations, encouragement and love, and a fun night of dancing! Tebow Time used to mean Tebow making plays on the field to help his team win, but now it's all about Tebow using his time on earth to leave a legacy for others.

Give People Great Stories to Tell

Lisa Rose, the creator of First Fridays in Dallas, met a woman named Deborah Lyons, who had created a program to help women and children in abusive relationships to leave the situation and become independent. Deborah had the program but needed the resources and a location to make it happen. So Lisa recruited her husband Matt, the executive chairman of BNSF Railway, to join her in this mission. Together they raised enough money to build The Gatehouse, consisting of 96 luxurious apartments on 60 acres of land in Grapevine, Texas, where they house, feed, encourage, mentor, counsel, and invest in women and their children who are escaping abusive situations. Residents, who are called members, have to work in jobs outside the community while living there, as they learn to provide for themselves, save money, and live independently. The average stay is about two years. Lisa said it's a place and a program for permanent change. "Everything we do is designed to provide them with a safe and comfortable place and then our program is designed to help them grow and create permanent change in their lives. It's not a shelter. It's a community. It's not a hand out. It's a hand up." I asked her if she modeled it after another program and she said, "There was nothing like it, so we had to create the model." They don't seek government funding. They raise all the money from businesses and private donors.

When Lisa showed me around the community, the education center, the chapel, the general store, the walking trails, and so on, she shared how they were currently raising an endowment that would help fund their yearly budget to ensure that The Gatehouse would continue long after she and Matt were gone. I was blown away. They are not only investing their lives to help people, but they are making sure they will still be making a difference after their death. When I left The Gatehouse, humbled by the experience, I couldn't help but think of all the children and future children living there and how, when they are older, they'll be telling their children stories about how Lisa, Matt, Deborah,

Positive Leaders Lead with Purpose

and The Gatehouse changed the course of their lives. You won't live forever, but your impact on others lives on after you are gone. You don't have to build a physical community like Lisa, Matt, and Deborah, but you can create a community wherever you are. One's legacy is carried on through love shared, lives touched, and stories told. The people you lead will be telling stories about you years from now. You can't escape it. They will be telling stories, so give people great stores to tell about you.

Life and Death

Nothing clarifies your purpose like a near-death experience. I don't recommend one, but it does work. A few years ago my family and I were on a plane from LAX Los Angeles heading to Atlanta. Shortly after taking off and soaring above 10,000 feet, the plane abruptly slowed down and the power went out as the pilot spoke over the sound system, "We're experiencing a mechanical failure and heading back for an emergency landing." The next moment the plane descended so rapidly that my head hurt and I thought we were going down. I looked at my wife and son, who were sitting to the left and a few rows back because we couldn't get seats together, and I saw the fear in my wife's eyes. I grabbed my daughter's hand as she sat in the seat directly in front of me.

This can't be happening, I thought. We're not ready to die. I still have three more books that I know I'm meant to write (this being one of them). A few minutes later, the plane leveled off as I watched off-duty airline employees, who were sitting in passenger seats, get up and run to the back of the plane. The pilot announced that we were going to make the emergency landing and to brace for impact. He said there would be emergency vehicles there to meet us and that the flight attendants were trained on what to do when we landed. While everything seemed eerily calm and quiet, I couldn't stop thinking about the plane catching on fire or splitting in two when we landed. Miraculously and thankfully, we made a safe landing. The pilot said there was a fire in one of the engines, so he descended rapidly to extinguish the fire in the same way that one breathes to blow out a candle.

When we walked off the plane, my 14-year-old son put his arm around me and said, "God's not done with us yet. It means we have more work to do." He was right. I left that experience more inspired than ever to live my purpose and leave a legacy with my life. I had more work to do and, if you are reading this, so do you. As a leader, you have more people to inspire, help, encourage, mentor, love, serve, and care for. You have more teams to lead and more people to impact. You have a world to change because the world needs a leader like you to change it.

Chapter 11

Positive Leaders Have Grit

*The number one predictor and factor of success
is not talent, title, wealth, or appearance. It is grit!*

A ngela Duckworth's research at the University of Pennsylvania identifies grit as the number-one predictor and factor of success. It's not talent, title, wealth, or good looks. It's grit, the ability to work hard for a long period of time towards a goal; to persevere, overcome, and keep moving forward in the face of adversity, failure, rejection, and obstacles.[16] Success doesn't happen overnight. Anything worthwhile takes time to build. Along the way a leader will face countless challenges, failures, and setbacks that will become roadblocks unless they find a way forward. Positive leaders have grit and find a way to navigate the roadblocks or run through them to move closer to their vision and goal.

When we look at successful companies and organizations, we see their current success and prominence but what we don't see is the leadership and grit that powered them through all the failure and moments of doubt, heartache, fear, and pain. Everyone would now like to be Kevin Plank, the CEO of Under Armour, but I'm guessing they wouldn't have wanted to be him in 1995 when he was selling one product, a new high-performance t-shirt, from the basement of his grandmother's home in Washington, DC, and financing his venture with a $40,000 loan from his maxed-out credit cards. Everyone would love to enjoy the success Sara Blakely, the owner of Spanx, has created, but I'm sure most wouldn't want to sell fax machines door to door at the age of 25, or go to North Carolina to visit most of the hosiery mills in the country to try to sell an idea for a new kind of undergarment. Most of us wouldn't have continued after being rejected by every representative. But she moved forward, and eventually found a manufacturer who agreed to make her product because his daughters thought it was a great idea. And with a lot of grit, she was able to transform the pantyhose industry and become the youngest self-made billionaire in history. Starbucks did not reach its fifth store until 13 years into its history. Sam Walton did not open his second store until seven years after starting his company. Pat Summitt, the legendary women's basketball coach at Tennessee, didn't win her first championship until her 13th year of coaching. Dabo Swinney and Clemson lost 15 of their first 34 games and went 6–7 in 2010. Dabo thought he was going to be fired but Clemson's athletic director at the time, Terry Don Phillips, shared his continued belief in him. After that, they won at least 10 games every year and a championship in 2016. And John Wooden didn't win his first national title until his 16th season at UCLA.

Whether you are attempting to turn around a company, grow a start-up, build a winning team, or move a successful organization to the next level, you can expect it to take time and perseverance. Duckworth says, "Grit is passion and perseverance for long-term goals." I would add that it's actually a marathon and a series of sprints combined with a boxing match. You are not just running but also getting hit along the way. Grit keeps you moving forward through the sting of rejection, pain of failure, and struggle with adversity. When life knocks you down, you may want to stay down and give up, but grit won't let you quit. This begs the question, "Why does grit keep you moving forward? How does it work? If grit drives you, what drives grit?"

Know What You Want

I believe true grit starts with knowing what you truly want. When you know what you want and you can see it, you will work hard and persevere in order to achieve it. That's why having a vision for the road ahead is so important. That's why we discussed the importance of a leader carrying a telescope and microscope with them. When the world doesn't see what you see and they think you are crazy for seeing it, your vision of what you want and the grit to keep going must be greater than all the negativity and naysayers. Sara Blakely said that she must have gotten hundreds of NO's along the way, but that didn't stop her. She knew what she wanted to create, believed in it, and kept working until people finally saw what she saw and understood her brilliant idea.

Know Your Why

In the last chapter we discussed the power of purpose. Well, it not only fuels positivity, but it also drives grit in a big way. When you know your *why*, you won't let obstacles get in your way. When your purpose is greater than your challenges, you won't give up. My dad was a New York City police officer. Each day he left the house, my mom feared that he wouldn't come home. He risked his life every day. Why? Was it the paycheck?

Not at all. He didn't make much but he worked for a bigger purpose. When crime and my mom made him want to quit, he wouldn't. He had a duty and a purpose to make New York a safer place, and that kept him going.

Love It

If you don't love it, you'll never be great at it. If you don't love it, you won't work to overcome all the challenges to keep doing it. If you love what you do, you won't quit when the world says you should. You will continue to show up every day, do the work, and discover that success is not created by other people's opinions. It's not created by what the media and fearful news say. It's not created by any of the circumstances outside you. It's created by the love you have inside you—love for what you do, for your team, for the organization you serve, and for the world you want to change. The love and grit that you possess on the inside will create the life you experience on the outside.

Love powers grit, and it also powers you over fear. I've heard it said that fear is the second most powerful force in the universe because it's the one thing that can keep us from our vision, goals, and dreams. Thankfully, there's a force more powerful than fear, and it is love. People think that fear is strong and love is weak, but love is more powerful than fear. We don't run into burning buildings because of fear. We do it because of love. Love is the antidote to fear. Love casts out fear so where there is love, fear dissipates. When I speak to leaders, coaches, and athletes, I encourage them to focus on the love of their work, craft, and competition instead of their fear of failing. Fear is draining, but love is sustaining. Fear causes you to worry

172

about what everyone will think if you fail. Love moves you to give your best and not worry about the rest. A field-goal kicker I know in the NFL was struggling during his second year after having a phenomenal rookie season. I reached out to him and asked what was going on. He said he was thinking too much. I said tell me about your rookie season. He said he was just thrilled to be in the NFL. He was living his dream and loving kicking. I said tell me about this year. He said he missed a few kicks in the pre-season and started to worry about missing. He didn't want to let the coach and team down. He didn't want to lose his job. I knew this problem well. Many people think that the more success you have, the less fear you have but, actually, it often works the other way. The more success you have, the more fear you have because you have more to lose and further to fall. I encouraged the field-goal kicker to get back to just loving the game, loving kicking, and loving the process. I told him to look inside, not outside. Just kick. Don't think. Just love it, don't fear it. He listened, was able to return to love, and had a great rest of the season. It wasn't me. I just reminded him what he already knew. I helped him to love it and, if you love it, you won't fear it. Most of all, if you love the process, you'll love what the process produces.

Embrace Failure

A big part of positive leadership and grit is knowing that you will fail along the way but you don't allow failure to define you or stop you. Failure is a big part of your path to success. It's not your enemy. It is your partner in growth. It doesn't define you; it refines you. If you didn't fail, you wouldn't build the character you need to succeed. When you have grit, you fail and you move forward. You see it as an event, not a definition. You leave the past and let it go. The path to greatness is never behind you. Just keep moving forward. Failure and challenges are just part of the journey. There's no accomplishment without struggle. No triumph without tests and failures along the way. There would be no stories of positive leaders changing the world if they didn't have to overcome adversity and failure in order to do so. So the next time you fail, remember that George Washington lost two thirds of all the battles he fought but won the Revolutionary War. Abraham Lincoln suffered nine election defeats, the death of a spouse, a nervous breakdown, and two bankruptcies before becoming President of the United States. Oprah was told she wasn't fit for television and was fired from her job as a news anchor. Walt Disney was fired from a newspaper job for a lack of ideas. Dr. Seuss wanted to burn the manuscript of his first book after it was rejected by 27 publishers. Steven Spielberg wasn't accepted to UCLA film school because of average grades. Phil Knight was on the brink of bankruptcy with Nike for over 10 years and routinely didn't know if the company could make payroll. Steve Jobs was fired from Apple at age 30, and the list goes on. You have to be willing to fail in order to succeed.

Keep Doing Things the Right Way: Trust the Process

David Cutcliffe, the head football coach at Duke, told me that when the team's record was 3–9 in 2010 and 2011 he felt optimistic because he knew what he was building and knew that they were doing things the right way. Then from 2012 to

2015 Duke made it to three straight postseason bowl games. I've had similar conversations with my friends and college lacrosse coaches John Tillman (Maryland), Jeff Tambroni (Penn State), Kevin Corrigan (Notre Dame), and Nick Myers (Ohio State). All of them have taken over programs and had to build them. The common denominator is to keep doing things the right way, even when the results aren't showing up yet. Don't focus on the numbers. Trust the process. When you keep doing things the right way, eventually the numbers will rise, the wins will come, and the outcome will happen.

Ignore the Critics; Do the Work

Positive leaders don't lead because they want recognition or enemies. They lead because there is something they must do, build, create, transform, and change. They lead because it's who they are and what they are meant to do. However, with leadership comes scrutiny, praise, critics, and attacks. A leader could find a cure for cancer and would still have some people criticize them for it. There was even once a leader who transformed the world by feeding the hungry, healing the sick, and loving the unlovable, and yet he was killed for it. If you are a leader, expect to be attacked. Positive leadership doesn't mean you won't be criticized. It means you have the grit and belief to overcome it. Positive leaders don't lead in a tranquil sea of positivity, but through the storms of adversity and negativity. Leadership is knowing that the critics will criticize you while still saying what needs to be said and doing what needs to be done. History doesn't remember the critic. It remembers the one who withstood criticism to accomplish something great.

In our modern social-media–driven world, you will have more fans and critics than ever. The keys are: Don't let praise go to your head and don't let critics into your head. Be so invested in your craft that you don't have time to listen to the naysayers. No time for negativity. You're too busy creating the future. If I would have listened to the naysayers and critics, I would have stopped working on my craft years ago. I want to encourage you to never let the opinion of others define you and your future. Your identity doesn't come from what the world says about you. It comes from who you are on the inside. Your work, leadership, and mission are too important to allow others to define your destiny.

No matter what anyone says, just show up and do the work.

If they praise you, show up and do the work.

If they criticize you, show up and do the work.

If no one even notices you, just show up and do the work.

Just keep showing up, doing the work, and leading the way.

Lead with passion.

Fuel up with optimism.

Have faith.

Power up with love.

Maintain hope.

Be stubborn.

Fight the good fight.

Refuse to give up.

Ignore the critics.

Believe in the impossible.

Show up.

Do the work.

You'll be glad you did.

True grit leads to true success.

Chapter 12

Lead the Way Forward

The best is yet to come.

I n this book I've shared stories of positive leaders who have transformed their teams and organizations and changed the world. I've also shared examples of positive leaders who are changing the world as we speak. In a world where there seems to be more negativity than ever, what gives me hope is that every week I meet and hear from new and emerging positive leaders. They remind me that we don't have to settle for the status quo and allow negative situations and circumstances to continue and exist. We don't have to be stuck in a negative rut. We don't have to allow negativity to rule our lives and our teams. Today we can decide to address problems, find solutions, and find a way forward. I don't know how old you are, where you are from, or anything about your career, experience, title, challenges, or how many people you lead, but I do know that today you can be the positive leader you were born to be. People often ask me if leadership is nature or nurture. Are you born a leader or can you develop into a leader? I believe you have everything you need inside you to be a positive leader. Life and circumstances don't make you into a leader. They reveal the leader you already are.

You don't have to change jobs to be a positive leader. You can be like Tanya Walters, who was a school bus driver in Los

Angeles. I met her while speaking in California. One day, after realizing that most of her students were failing in school, Tanya decided to challenge them to do better. She challenged them to study harder, focus more, and improve their grades. When they succeeded, she took them on a marine biology cruise, which led to the idea of a summer bus trip around the country. The purpose was to expose children to a world and life beyond the toughest streets in Los Angeles. She succeeded and now, many trips later, her non-profit, GodParents Youth Organization, has evolved into a powerful mentoring and touring program that takes children to colleges and historical sites around the country. It was even featured on *Oprah*. Tanya could have just continued driving the bus and ignored the challenges her students were facing. Instead, she chose to commit her life and work to showing them the world, and she's changing lives in the process. She chose to be a driver of positive change and instead of letting the world influence her, she's a positive leader who is influencing the world.

You can also be like Ursula, who was a pharmacy tech for a large drugstore chain. She told me she was a single mom who had been through a lot of hardships in her life but prided herself on her passion for her job. However, after transferring to the roughest store in the city, her passion quickly fizzled as she dealt with all the difficult customers and negativity in the pharmacy. She was ready to throw in the towel, but didn't want to leave a job she loved. After reading a few of my books, she decided her purpose was "To provide selfless service to her coworkers and customers and to make it a fun and uplifting environment." She said she brought in a huge pot of queso dip just because it was so good and everyone loved it. Then she and her team started listening to upbeat music and the atmosphere—as well as everyone's attitudes—changed instantly. She said, "It was so fun! The difficult customers I used to dread serving are now opportunities for me to shine. My goal is to make sure they leave my presence with a smile on their face. I help my coworkers at every chance I get and I make sure I try to lift them up with encouragement and compliments. I even leave little gifts for them, like a compliment on a sticky note for the new guy or a little picked flower for another single mom. I am loving my job again, I'm living in the moment, and my passion is back!" Ursula didn't need to change her job. She just needed to change her attitude, and in the process she changed everyone around her.

You don't have to continue living life in a negative rut. You can be like me and so many of the people I have met who have gone from negative to positive. My friend Rachel, for example, wouldn't stop complaining to me at a party. For 20 minutes she bombarded me with a series of complaints. She complained about her job. She complained about her company's new policies. She complained about the economy. Most of all she complained about her lack of sales. I wanted to say something but I couldn't get a word in. Finally I stopped her and told her she had a choice. "You can accept your company's new policies, come to work with a positive attitude, and decide to be your best every day or you can find a new job at a new company. But whatever you do, stop complaining because it's not doing you any good." The conversation was over and so was our friendship, I thought, because Rachel wouldn't speak to me for a few months. Then my wife and I saw her at the grocery store and she told me that while it was hard to hear what I had to say, she had decided to take my advice. She stayed in her job, stopped complaining, and started selling more. Three months after changing her attitude, her sales were up 30 percent. A year later, her sales were up 70 percent. Three years after our initial conversation, I caught up with Rachel again. We hadn't spoken in a long time and I was wondering how she was doing. Rachel told me that during the last two years her sales continued to grow. She has been promoted twice and is now in her dream job, leading a division at her company. It's the job she always wanted and she's more excited and passionate than ever about her work. Rachel stopped whining and started *winning*!

Andy Green was a young third-base coach for the Arizona Diamondbacks, but because of the way he invested in relationships with his players, worked hard, served others, and led with optimism and belief, he caught the eye of the owners and general managers of other teams and was hired to be the manager of the San Diego Padres. Andy said he wasn't always about other people. As a young baseball player, he was all about his own career advancement, but after being released by the Cincinnati Reds, he told his wife that if he ever got the opportunity to play Major League Baseball again, it would be about others and not himself. He got another shot to play in the big leagues with the Mets and he became a leader in the clubhouse and eventually a minor league manager, where he won back-to-back Manager of the Year awards before joining the Diamondbacks as a coach. Andy's career highlight wasn't his major-league debut or game-winning home run, but rather knocking on one of his minor league players' hotel room door at one o'clock in the morning and telling him that he was going to the big leagues for the first time. The player cried like a baby, Andy hugged him and years later Andy said so far he hasn't had a better highlight than that. I spoke to Andy's team last year and his players told me he's genuine, caring, selfless, and always looking for ways to help them improve in baseball and life. He's a positive leader who decided to make a difference wherever he was and, as a result, he's now leading at the highest level of his profession. I've worked with countless coaches who have been hired, promoted, and built great careers and teams because of their positive leadership. Some were already positive leaders. Some became positive leaders and it made all the difference.

While you don't have to leave your job to be a positive leader, for some people it does require a change in location, career, and calling. You may have to leave the old behind in order to create the new. Niki Spears was a principal of a school in Fort Bend when she reached out to me and said she wanted to take *The Energy Bus* message to schools around the world and create an Energy Bus for Schools program. Over the years I have had a number of people approach me about this idea, but once they realized the commitment it would take to make it happen, their enthusiasm gave way to reality and they decided against moving forward. I wanted to see it happen because I had a vision for it but knew it would take the right person. When Niki approached me I thought she would be like the others and fade away, but she didn't. She shared the same vision and was so committed to it that she left her job as a principal with no guarantee of success or a salary, and has since created a movement of Energy Bus Schools that are transforming negativity in schools and helping develop positive leaders for the future. I've watched her grow from a principal of one school to now a leader of leaders who is helping tens of thousands of educators and students improve and grow. She tapped into the power of positive leadership and now she's transforming the lives of principals, teachers, students, and their families. She's still an educator. She's just educating many schools and classrooms instead of one.

You may have to leave everything behind to become the leader you are meant to be. You may be like Scott Harrison, who was a night club promoter, drank heavily, smoked two packs of cigarettes a day, often woke up hungover, and was one of the top club promoters in New York City. Scott was at the top of his game, but one day he realized he was playing the wrong game. He didn't want to rally people to meet at bars. He wanted to unite people to make a difference. That ultimately led to visits to Africa, where he discovered that each day 1,400 children die from diseases caused by unsafe water and poor sanitation. Scott learned that women and children will walk miles, sometimes taking half a day, to find drinking water when there's fresh, clean water available in the ground right under their feet in their village. All that's needed is a well to extract the water and the funds to install it. Scott created Charity Water to fill this need, and he started rallying many of his friends he met through his years promoting nightclubs. Early on, Scott was having trouble raising money to keep the non-profit running, and he refused to use money he had raised to install water wells on operations. He was a few weeks away from closing down Charity Water when a donor gave him a million dollars to keep it going for another year. Scott said that at the time he thought the money was what kept him going but, looking back, he realizes it was the belief. Now, years later, instead of watching people get drunk, he's providing people around the world with water to drink—and saving lives and transforming communities in the process. To date, Charity Water has helped provide 7 million people with clean drinking water and continues to help provide water to 2,700 new people every day.

Yes, there's a lot of negativity in the world. Yes, there are many problems that haven't been solved yet. But instead of focusing on all that's wrong, you can realize that this is your time to make things right. With all the negativity in the world, what a great opportunity you have to be a positive leader and influencer. With all the technology and resources, there's never been a better time to make a positive difference. When Alan Mulally was contemplating becoming the CEO of Ford, despite all the extreme challenges the company was facing, he did his homework and knew all the daunting tasks that lie ahead, but he didn't run from it. When writing notes to himself about the prospect of becoming the CEO of Ford and turning it around, he wrote, "Wow. What fun!" He knew it was a big problem that only a great leader could solve and he was up to the task to try.

Your circumstances might be difficult and daunting and so were Austin Hatch's. He was a rising star in Fort Wayne, Indiana, with a scholarship to play basketball at Michigan when, while flying with his dad and stepmother on a private plane, the plane crashed. His father and stepmother were both killed and Austin suffered life-threatening injuries and brain trauma. He was in a coma for a month. It was a horrible tragedy made worse by the fact that Austin had lost his mother and two siblings in another crash that he and his father had

Lead the Way Forward

survived years before. Austin has the rare distinction of being someone who has survived two plane crashes. The odds of this happening are 11 quadrillion, 5 trillion to one. Yet as miraculous as this was, the doctors believe it was even more miraculous that Austin not only walked again but graduated high school, attended Michigan, and joined the basketball team, which honored his scholarship. Austin can't play like he used to, but his leadership is a huge asset to his coach and Michigan teammates. While talking to Austin on the phone recently, he told me about not letting circumstances define him. He said he made a decision in the hospital while trying to walk again that he would do whatever it took to walk out of that hospital. He said he wanted to be a miracle for others. He said, "My life is only a miracle if I can be a miracle to others." And now, as a sophomore at Michigan, he's finding time between studying and basketball to share and inspire others with his message. He's living to be a miracle for others and so can you.

Nick called me a few days ago. He's a young man in the insurance business. We've actually never met. I spoke to his company's leadership last year and his boss told me about him and how he was struggling, and I said I would call and encourage him. I called him and he was a really nice young man just going through a lot of internal struggles. I had him read one of my books and then said we would talk about what he had learned. We did this once a month for a few months and then I didn't hear from him for a while. When he called me the other day out of the blue he told me about the holidays and how his positive attitude had helped him have a great time with his family. He said where there used to be strife with his siblings there was now meaningful conversation and connection. He said because he had changed, everything around him seemed to change, including his career, which is thriving. Most significant of all, Nick told me that his best friend's dad had died, but because Nick had grown as a leader, he was able to be there for his friend and help him through this difficult time. "That would never have happened last year," he said. "I would have fallen apart and everyone would have had to help me. But now I was able to help him." Nick was able to be a miracle to his friend and family.

That's how it works. Your one decision to be a positive leader will not only impact your life, but your relationships, your family, your friends, and your team. A life touches a life that touches a life. A person changes and they help others change. A leader inspires others and develops more leaders. The seed you plant today becomes the harvest you enjoy tomorrow. You may not see the harvest but don't let that stop you from planting the seeds. There are seeds to plant, lives to change, teams to transform, problems to solve, and a world to change. When you become a positive leader, you will not only make yourself better, but you will also make everyone around you better—and that's a great place to start!

Notes

1. Puri, M. & Robinson, D. (2007). Optimism and economic choice. *Journal of Financial Economics*, 86, 71-99.

2. Seligman, M.E. & Schulman, P. (1986). Explanatory style as a predictor of productivity and quitting among life insurance sales agents. *Journal of Personality and Social Psychology*, 50(4), 832–838.

3. Fredrickson, B. (2001). The role of positive emotions in positive psychology: The broaden-and-build theory of positive emotions. *American Psychologist*, 56, 218-226.

4. Goleman, D. (2011). *Leadership: The power of emotional intelligence*. Florence, MA: More Than Sound Publishers.

5. Gottman, J. (1994). *Why marriages succeed or fail*. New York, NY: Simon & Schuster.

6. Baker, W., Cross, R., & Wooten, M. (2003). Positive organizational network analysis and energizing relationships. In J. Cameron, J.E. Dutton, & R. Quinn (Eds.), *Positive Organizational Scholarship: Foundations of a New Discipline* (pp. 328-342). San Francisco, CA: Berrett-Koehler Publishers, Inc.

7. McCraty, R., Atkinson, M., Tomasino, D., & Tiller, W. (1998). The electricity of touch: Detection and measurement of cardiac energy exchange between people. In Karl H. Pribram (Eds.), *Brain Values: Is a Biological Science of*

Values Possible? Mahwah, NJ: Lawrence Erlbaum Associates, 359-379.

8. Fowler, J. & Christakis, N. (2008). Dynamic spread of happiness in a large social network: Longitudinal analysis over 20 years in the Framingham Heart Study. *British Medical Journal*, 337(no. a2338), 1-9.

9. Croft, A., Dunn, E., & Quoidbach, J. (2014). From tribulations to appreciation: Experiencing adversity in the past predicts greater savoring in the present. *Social Psychological and Personality Science*, 5(5), 511-516.

10. Reptilian coping brain. (2017). Retrieved from http://www. copingskills4kids.net/Reptilian_Coping_Brain.html

11. Rowland, K. A. (2008). *The relationship of principal leadership and teacher morale.* (Doctoral dissertation). Retrieved from ProQuest.

12. Cocksedge, S., George, B., Renwick, S., & Chew-Graham, C.A. (2013). Touch in primary care consultations: Qualitative investigation of doctors' and patients' perceptions. *The British Journal of General Practice*, 63(609), 283–290.

13. Rath, Tom (2007). *Strengths Finder 2.0*. Gallup Press.

14. Wrzesniewski, A., Schwartz, B., Cong, X., Kane, M., Omar, A., & Kolditz, T. (2014). Multiple types of motives don't multiply the motivation of West Point cadets. *Proceedings of the National Academy of Sciences*, 111(30), 10990–10995.

15. Campolo, T. (2008). *Letters to a young evangelical*. Basic Books.

16. Duckworth, A. & Peterson, C. (2007). Grit: Perseverance and passion for long-term goals. *Journal of Personality and Social Psychology*, 92(6), 1087-1101.

ACKNOWLEDGMENTS

Every book I've written has taken four weeks or less to write and I don't take credit for that. I'm thankful to God for the inspiration, ideas, ability, and wisdom to write books. I'm thankful for my wife, Kathryn, and her continued support and belief. I appreciate Ken Blanchard for being a mentor and a role model for me. He and his mentor Norman Vincent Peale were the pioneers of the *Power of Positive Leadership*. Thank you to Daniel Decker for being a great friend, business partner, and team member. Thank you to Shannon Vargo and Matt Holt at John Wiley and Sons for taking a chance on me and *The Energy Bus* years ago. It's been an amazing ride. Thanks to Elizabeth Gildea, Deborah Schindlar, and Peter Knox for your help getting the book published and promoted. Thank you to Patrick Lencioni, Jeff Gibson, and Amy Hiett for introducing me to Alan Mulally. Thank you to Alan Mulally for your incredible example, wisdom, and insights regarding Positive Leadership. I feel like I earned an MBA from our conversation. Thank you to Dabo Swinney for your friendship and opportunity to work with Clemson football over the years. It's been an incredible, meaningful, rewarding, and spiritual journey. I've learned so much from you. Thank you to Doug Conant, Dave Roberts, Donna Orender, Shawn Eichorst, Sandy Barbour, Mike Smith, Carl Liebert, Cori Close, Brendan Suhr, Billy Donovan, Doc Rivers, Kevin Eastman, Sherri Coale, Erik Spoelstra, John

Calipari, Mark Richt, Clint Hurdle, Kyle Stark, Butch Jones, Tara VanDerveer, Andy Green, Drew Watkins, Rick Hendrick, John Desmond, Chad Knaus, Boo Corrigan, David Cutcliffe, John Tillman, Jeff Tambroni, Chip Kelly, Gus Bradley, Buzz Williams, Chad Morris, Christine Halfpenny, Rhonda Revelle, Steve Gilbert and George Raveling for the opportunity to work with your teams, learn from you, and see Positive Leadership in action. Thank you to Jim Van Allan for your help with research. Thank you to Joshua Medcalf for challenging me to make the book better. Thank you to my brother David Gordon for your input and ideas. Thank you to Kate Leavell, Julie Nee, Amy Kelly, Brett Hughes, Anne Carlson, and Brooke Trabert for reading the book and offering feedback. Thank you to all the great leaders and companies who give me the opportunity to work with your organizations and teams. Thank you to all the positive leaders who make everyone around them better. Together we will change the world!

Bring the Power of Positive Leadership to Your Organization

KEYNOTE

VIDEO PROGRAM

ACTION PLAN

OFFSITE

Visit www.PowerofPositiveLeadership.com
or call 904-285-6842 for more information.

Power of Positive Leadership Resources

Visit www.PowerofPositiveLeadership.com for:

Action Plans

Posters

Video Program

Training

If you are interested in contacting Jon Gordon and his team, please contact The Jon Gordon Companies at:

Phone: 904-285-6842

E-mail: info@jongordon.com

Online: JonGordon.com

Twitter: @JonGordon11

Facebook: Facebook.com/JonGordonpage

Instagram: JonGordon11

Sign up for Jon's weekly positive tip at: JonGordon.com.

Other Books by Jon Gordon

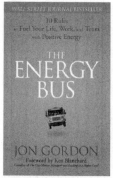

The Energy Bus

A man whose life and career are in shambles learns from a unique bus driver and set of passengers how to overcome adversity. Enjoy this enlightening ride of positive energy that is improving the way leaders lead, employees work, and teams function.

www.TheEnergyBus.com

The Energy Bus for Kids

This illustrated children's adaptation of the bestselling book *The Energy Bus* tells the story of George, who, with the help of his school bus driver Joy, learns that if he believes in himself, he'll find the strength to overcome any challenge. His journey teaches kids how to overcome negativity, bullies, and everyday challenges to be their best.

www.EnergyBusKids.com

The No Complaining Rule

Follow a VP of human resources who must save herself and her company from ruin, and discover proven principles and an actionable plan to win the battle against individual and organizational negativity.

www.NoComplainingRule.com

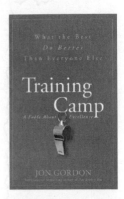

Training Camp

This inspirational story about a small guy with a big heart and a special coach who guides him on a quest for excellence reveals the eleven winning habits that separate the best individuals and teams from the rest.

www.TrainingCamp11.com

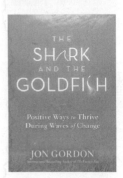

The Shark and the Goldfish

Delightfully illustrated, this quick read is packed with tips and strategies for responding to challenges beyond your control in order to thrive during waves of change.

www.SharkandGoldfish.com

Soup

The newly anointed CEO of a popular soup company is brought in to reinvigorate the brand and bring success back to a company that has fallen on hard times. Through her journey, discover the key ingredients to unite, engage, and inspire teams and create a culture of greatness.

www.Soup11.com

The Seed

Go on a quest for the meaning and passion behind work with Josh, an up-and-comer at his company who is disenchanted with his job. Through Josh's cross-country journey, you'll find surprising new sources of wisdom and inspiration in your own business and life.

www.Seed11.com

The Positive Dog

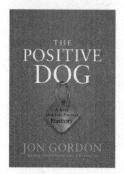

We all have two dogs inside of us. One dog is positive, happy, optimistic, and hopeful. The other dog is negative, mad, pessimistic, and fearful. These two dogs often fight inside us, but guess who wins the fight? The one you feed the most. *The Positive Dog* is an inspiring story that not only reveals the strategies and benefits of being positive but also highlights an essential truth for humans: Being positive doesn't just make you better. It makes everyone around you better.

www.feedthepositivedog.com

The Carpenter

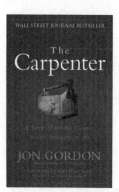

The Carpenter is Jon Gordon's most inspiring book yet — filled with powerful lessons and the greatest success strategies of all. Michael wakes up in the hospital with a bandage on his head and fear in his heart, after collapsing while on a morning jog. When Michael finds out the man who saved his life is a Carpenter, he visits him and quickly learns that he is more than just a Carpenter; he is also a builder of lives, careers, people, and teams. In this journey, you will learn the timeless principles to help you stand out, excel, and make an impact on people and the world.

www.carpenter11.com

The Hard Hat

A true story about Cornell lacrosse player George Boiardi, *The Hard Hat* is an unforgettable book about a selfless, loyal, joyful, hard-working, competitive, and compassionate leader and teammate, the impact he had on his team and program, and the lessons we can learn from him. This inspirational story will help you discover how to be the best teammate you can be and how to build a great team.

www.hardhat21.com

You Win in the Locker Room First: The 7 C's to Build a Winning Team in Business, Sports, and Life

Based on the extraordinary experiences of NFL Coach Mike Smith and leadership expert Jon Gordon, *You Win in the Locker Room First* offers a rare, behind-the-scenes look at one of the most pressure-packed leadership jobs on the planet and what leaders can learn from these experiences in order to build their own winning team.

wininthelockerroom.com

Other Books by Jon Gordon